A Handful of Flowers

A brief biography of Buton Rinpoche

by
Dratshadpa Rinchen Namgyal

Translated by
Hans van den Bogaert

LIBRARY OF TIBETAN WORKS AND ARCHIVES

First edition 1996

ISBN: 81-86470-04-2

Published by the Library of Tibetan Works & Archives, Dharamsala 176215, India, and printed at Indraprastha Press (CBT), Nehru House, New Delhi-110002.

CONTENTS

Foreword

Tibet's rich and ancient culture has owed a great debt to significant individuals down the centuries. There is now a growing body of literature in translation about these enlightened masters and historical figures. This English translation of the condensed biography of Buton Rinpoche is a welcome addition.

Buton Rinpoche (1290–1364) became one of Tibet's most renowned scholars and translators. His life and work are notable for the effort he made to honour all the orders and systems of tenets of Tibetan Buddhism.

This account of Buton Rinpoche's life by Dratshadpa Rinchen Namgyal recounts many of his great compassionate activities. It is a source of wisdom and inspiration for Buddhist practitioners even today.

I congratulate the translator, Hans van den Bogaert, and everyone who has contributed to making the biography of this exemplary master available to interested persons who do not read Tibetan.

May 7, 1996

THE DALAI LAMA

Publisher's Note

A Handful of Flowers is a condensed biography of the 14th-century Buddhist scholar and master, Buton Rinchen Drub. In translation it offers a valuable addition to the body of works, rendered into English, of outstanding historical figures in the Buddhist world.

Born in the year 1290, Buton Rinpoche showed extraordinary qualities from a young age, and grew up to become one of Tibet's greatest and most prolific scholars and translators. Acting always out of boundless compassion, and with inestimable wisdom, he worked tirelessly for the liberation of all sentient beings. He became known as the Lord of Zhalu—amongst other eminent titles—Zhalu being the location of his principal monastery and retreat centre.

This biography was composed as a hymn of praise to his master by the monk-disciple Dratshadpa Rinchen Namgyal. It has been ably translated into English by Hans van den Bogaert, who is to be commended for his devotion and the thoroughness of his endeavors. May the merit gained by publishing this inspirational life-story be shared among all sentient beings, and bring them benefit.

Gyatsho Tshering
Director

June 1996

Introduction

Namo Gurubhya!

This is the biography called *A Handful of Flowers*, which narrates some events from the life of the great scholar, the all-knowing translator Buton Rinpoche.

With great respect I bow down at the feet of the holy master, who is the essential nature of all the Buddhas of the three times, a precious treasure of all qualities of virtue and excellence, a spiritual friend who protects the multitudes of transmigrating beings from suffering. I bow down at the feet of the Lord of Dharma, the learned and accomplished Buton Rinpoche.

The boundless collection of good qualities of this holy guide is in fact inexpressible. Even the Buddhas and Bodhisattvas would not be able to mention them all in eons or periods longer than that.

In a period long ago, this great person was a mighty Lord of the twelve stages[1] and reached Buddhahood with a Corpus of Complete Enjoyment (Sambhogakaya)[2] after which he manifested various Corpora of Emanations (Nirmanakaya).[3] Thus he simultaneously resided in the pure realm Tushita and took birth and played as a child and so on. With some of these (emanation bodies) he renounced worldly life and practiced austerities, he moved to Vajrasana,[4] where he sat down (to meditate) and subdued the Maras. He turned the Wheels of the Dharma and showed his entrance into Parinirvana.

In this way he still manifests himself in the pure realms with his Sambhogakaya and in the impure realms as medicines, bridges, birds, deer and the like, the common pure and impure (appearances). He sometimes took on the appearance of a Bodhisattva abiding on the stages, sometimes of a Chakravartin King,[5] of Brahma and of Indra, of siddhas and of pandita scholars and so forth.

In short, this great person appeared as a Buddha to beings to be subdued by a Buddha and as a Bodhisattva to beings to be tamed by a Bodhisattva.

Similarly he also appeared to each—a Shravaka[6] and a Pratyeka Arhat,[7] a deva, a naga, an asura, a sramanera, a Brahmin, a layman and so on, in the form of the one who is to train them, and took innumerable births with an ability to teach innumerable practices in innumerable languages to infinite beings, both human and non-human and placed them on the basis of the paths and the results.

I will narrate some of the actions of this great person where he temporarily took on ordinary appearances to act for the beings in this world. Once, when this great person was a salesman, he made a priceless offering of precious jewels to the Tathagata of Infinite Light (mtha' yas 'od) and first generated the supreme mind of enlightenment.

At another time, as the son of King Sonam Metog, he rejoiced when the Tathagata of Infinite Enthusiastic Perseverance (brtson 'grus mtha' yas) manifested the single-pointed concentration called the teaching of the certainty of infinite practices (chos kyi tshul nges par ston pa). With this appreciation he shortened his stay in cyclic existence by 80.000 eons and never again had any downfalls or experience of lack of leisure. He then obtained the dharani (gzungs) called: Chima can (phyi ma can).

It was prophesied that of the 1,000 Buddhas who will appear in this fortunate era, he will appear as the seventh Buddha to teach the Dharma. This was prophesied by the Siddha and Rishi of Ribo Jakang (China), the Siddha from Ugyan (Swat) and the Arhat from Sri Lanka unanimously. He also took birth in this world as a very learned pandita scholar of the South and due to him all the arguments of the outsiders, the Tithikas, were uprooted and overcome. As he lifted up the victory banner of the inner doctrine, Lord Buddha's doctrine flourished like a rising sun. It became very important and was able to greatly contribute to the well-being of many sentient beings.

He actually received teachings on the Abhisamayalankara[8] directly from the venerable protector Maitreya and upon extending his hand to Kashmir Maitreya instructed (the great scholar) to go to the East. He received transmissions from Shanta Akara and others and while seated in a bath of sesame oil he performed 100,000 recitations. At Sumpakuta he consulted Arya Tara about an answer to the arguments of the Tirthikas and received it. In the Malaya forest he heard the voices of Manjushri, Hayagriva and Tara.

When begging for alms, the shapes of an eternity knot, a conch-shell coiling to the right and a golden fish and other auspicious symbols appeared in his porridge.

When he taught the teachings of Maitreya at Magadha, the devas caused a rain of flowers to fall. At Vikramapuri (Vikramashila)[9] he was the principal of an assembly of 1,000 sangha members. At Odantapuri (Orissa)[10] an assembly of 11,000 sangha members paid respect to him. When he took a tambula in his hands to offer to the Buddha statue at Bodh Gaya, the statue smiled. When he was together with the Shravakas of Lord Buddha at Dawa Trampa (zla ba bkram pa), he saw a naga-snake raise its hood and offer alms. At Dzayakana (Jayapuri) he saw a Devaputra move a fan at a vision of Maitreya and he heard the seven Dharma teachings. In the bamboo forest ('dam bu'i tshal) while Kubera (Lnga rtsen) offered songs and praises, he accepted alms from a drawing of a girl, after which the porridge was transformed into nectar. When he lit lamps Lord Buddha, Maitreya and Tara were seen in the flames. When he stayed at Magadha, Arya Tara instructed him to go to the east and the north. When he listened to teachings on secret mantra from Devapuna, he clearly saw the appearance of the three Meditation Buddhas Hevajra, Heruka and Kalachakra together with their surrounding deities.

The Devaputras Ushnishavijaya (gtsug tor) and Namtö (rnam thos) advised him to go to the north, to Tibet where he was known as the Kashmiri Pandit. He became very famous and when he was 99 years old a staircase of light rays invited him to Tushita, which was witnessed by 200 pandits. It is well known from the words of the unrivalled and indescribable precious Bodhisattva Throphuba that he went to Tibet to subdue the beings there. He became very famous in this world.

In the great snowland of Tibet he took on the appearance of a Bodhisattva residing in the great stages, of a collector of the teachings, he took birth as a pandit scholar and translator who assembled and translated all the practices taught by Lord Buddha into the Tibetan language. Thus he greatly enhanced the practice of the doctrine. He upheld the great victory banner and made sure that the holy Dharma did not decline. He put an end to wrong practices of the doctrine and removed all the impurities of non-understanding and wrong understanding.

Teaching the profound path which is certain to lead to Buddhahood without any mistakes, he presented the marvellous appearance of ripening sentient beings and liberating them. Such illustrious appearances are difficult to fathom even for great saints and are extremely difficult to understand by childish beings like me, a fool whose eyes are covered with ignorance.

In this way (Buton Rinpoche) manifested the deeds of his

Nirmanakayas with inconceivable emanations in countless realms, due to his capacity to instantly radiate many (bodies) from one and to contract many into one and so forth. As it is impossible to narrate them all extensively and in detail, the above-mentioned are only a hint as to his former births and enlightened activities.

Chapter one

The birth of Buton Rinpoche in 1290 up to his retirement from Zhalu in 1356

Here follows the story of his birth and great deeds in his life as Buton Rinpoche, when this great person emanated an ordinary appearance corresponding to our common notions and showed the manner of practising the path.

He possessed clairvoyance without obstruction, seeing all the hidden things of the past and of the future very clearly as well as his births in previous existences. With his unobstructed clairvoyance he also saw that he would benefit the doctrine and many sentient beings if, in order to subdue the people of Tibet, he were to take birth in an ordinary body with Tibetan parents, with freedom from the eight non-freedoms, in a family neither too exalted nor too low. Thus he took birth in the precious place called Nyangro Nazhi (ngang ro sna bzhi rin po che'i gling).

His father was the glorious Lama Gyaltsen Pal Zangpo. He was well favored with many qualities and his family lineage called Brag had not suffered worldly defects for 17 generations. Known everywhere as Lama Brag Ton (brag ston), he was the head of a high and excellent family lineage including many who had attained realization in the practice of secret mantra in the Nyingmapa tradition and was famous for his knowledge of the scriptures and the meaning of mantra and (philosophical) definitions.

His mother was called Acharya Sönam Bum (slob dpon ma bsod nams 'bum). She was born in Shabmä Murtso (between Sakya and Shigatse). She was the daughter in a lineage of powerful and unequalled tantric practitioners—who had been holders of the practices of the secret mantra for many generations, who were learned in the teachings of the Nyingmapa tradition and had acquired profound spiritual power.

(Buton Rinpoche) took birth with this father and mother and when he entered the womb, his mother had a dream in which she experienced the generation of the supporting and supported mandala of her Meditation Buddha. The dream was so clear that she still experienced the bliss and emptiness when she woke up and many doors of single-pointed concentration arose in her mind. Her body felt blissful and light as if it had wings. As the months passed and he resided in her womb, he continually worked for the benefit of many sentient beings and placed them on the ground of liberation.

Then, in the year of the male iron tiger (1290), on the ninth day after the full moon of the middle spring month, under the constellation of the rooster, he took birth in the hermitage called the meditation place of Lower Shab (shab smad bsgom gnas). At that time his mother had a dream of him leaving the supporting and supported mandala of the Meditation Buddha to perform the general and specific deeds of purifying worlds, ripening beings and making offerings to the Buddhas and so on, after which she had a vision of his returning into the mandala.

At the time of his birth the air was filled with fragrant scents, pleasant music was heard and grasses and flowers which did not exist before grew outside. His birth was accompanied by the auspicious omen of good health, abundant harvests and happy times. He possessed a natural disposition for tranquility and discipline, clarity and prudence, conscientiousness, respect for the elderly and great compassion.

When he was still in the womb, his mother was took food that increases intelligence and she created many favorable conditions. Once he was born and started growing up, he meditated on Manjushri and received a vision of him. He said that ever afterwards, each time when he had to explain a Dharma practice he had not yet understood, all the words and the meaning would come very clearly to his mind, after sincerely reciting the praises and sadhana of Yeshe Zangpo's 'Praise of the good qualities of Manjushri'.

When he was five or six years old, his mother started to teach him to read. Whereas other children first had to learn the alphabet, she taught Buton by slowly reading the 'Daka Yeshe' and spelling it together with him. He memorized the 'Daka Yeshe' straightaway while reading along with her and astonished everyone. But as he did not easily understand the meaning while reading it with his mother, he said that she needed to teach him to read in such a way that he would easily understand the meaning as well. Soon he learned how to read by putting words together, without the need of others reading to him and thus he memorized 'The Sutra at the Request of Ksitigarbha' and even correctly understood the meaning of the words of the 'Daka Yeshe' which he had read before. When he wished to read the 'headless' script, he felt sad that he could not do so and wept. Then, by the waves of inspiration of the Meditation Buddha, he sighed and immediately he could read the 'headless' script out loud without any difficulty.

While all the children of his age studied to avoid punishment from their teachers, Buton learned to read very well even at times when there was no teacher around. The word spread that this special child who pleased all was in fact not an ordinary person. Even when he was still a young boy, he was not fond of amusements, but was very energetic in developing good qualities. He did not display any of the behavior of ordinary children.

His grandfather was an important lama called Tsultrim Pal Zangpo (bla chen tshul khrims dpal bzang po) who had visions of his Meditation Buddha and had acquired great powers as a physician. He also possessed single-pointed concentration on the profound meaning (nang ting nge 'dzin zab mo'i don) and had incredible capacities. Buton read all his books and understood all their meanings. He was able to differentiate between the commentaries which were completely pure and the ones which were not completely pure, and thereby greatly pleased his grandfather.

With the Lord Gyam Senge (dpon rgaum seng ge) who was an expert in the various sciences he studied astrology and grammar and he reached the state of a learned teacher.

When he was seven years old he met with the great Bodhisattva Trophuba Rinpoche and at that moment requested him for the generation of the Mahayana mind, and the mind of enlightenment which cherishes (all) others (more than oneself) was born in him. After he had asked for it again three times, he received great benefit. The thought then came to his mind:

If for the purpose of others,
Or for the purpose of the doctrine,
Or for the happiness of sentient beings,
I have to die, may I die!
If I have to suffer, may I suffer!

This verse of the mind of enlightenment is still recited today. At the beginning of each Dharma teaching he would gaze attentively at all those around him and he would close his eyes firmly now and then and did not lose his motivation even for a moment, while teaching the Dharma undistractedly. Without any effort he had a constant regard for the mind of enlightenment. To others he would say: "Oh yes, you should listen in order to attain Buddhahood for the purpose of all sentient beings," and he would repeat this even when teaching only a few lines. On top of that he always reflected: 'How can I become more effective for the purpose of all sentient beings?' In brief, even when dealing with worldly affairs and ordinary people, he maintained the vast path of the mind that considers others equal to oneself. This holy person had the power to not be distracted for even a moment from the precious mind of enlightenment which cherishes others more than oneself.

When he saw or heard stories about this contemporary world, where even intelligent people are preoccupied with having many attendants, are talkative, fond of wealth and therefore commit many negative deeds, he would shed tears from his eyes and generate great compassion. He felt compassion for each suffering being. "Because they wink with their eyes when they hear about death, they do not have the practices they need to cope at the time of death and they do not get another opportunity. Once they are confronted with the consequences of their deeds that lead them to hell, they are struck with panic. Still, because they enjoy what is in fact suffering, they take joy in the creation of even more causes of suffering. For all these beings I have compassion." Thus he said and he thought: 'How can I do something to benefit them?'

Whenever he heard that someone had died, he said, "Have mercy!" and would take an interest in the deceased person. It did not matter to him whether he had been requested to do so or not; he would take an interest anyway and engage in the practice of the profound inner and outer mandala for 49 days. These are all signs that he had received the power of the precious mind of enlightenment in his mind.

When he was invited by (low) laypeople such as fishermen or hunters, his attendants begged him not to go, saying that there would be defilements and that it was not suitable to go there. But he would reply: "As I have compassion for each suffering being, I have to go there in order to purify them from their defilements." He partook of the food there, spoke about good qualities and make dedications of offerings. In this way he installed faith in the Dharma.

In brief, he did many practices with the power of the precious mind of enlightenment, but as I fear writing too much, I will not write any more.

Buton Rinpoche often said that these manifestations of the mind of enlightenment were due to the kindness of the great Bodhisattva Throphuba. When he was eight years old, he requested the great Bodhisattva Throphuba Rinpoche for the four complete empowerments in the mandala of Chakrasamvara (bde mchog) according to the Sakya tradition of the Mahasiddha Ganthapada (Dril bu pa). Then Throphuba Rinpoche placed his hand on his head for a little while and spoke to him. "Oh, through him I can take a rest." It was at that time that he received the tantric vow of a knowledge holder (rig pa 'dzin pa'i sdom pa). Moreover, he received various profound Dharma instructions.

From his grandfather, the great Lama Tsultrim Pal Zangpo he heard 'The Tantra of the Secret Essence' (gsang ba snying po) and 'The Tantra of the Collected Meanings' (dgongs 'dus) and other tantras and commentaries such as the 'Par Khab' (spar khab). In brief, he received all the commentaries and expositions of the Nyingma (old) tradition of secret mantra without any exception, from the commentaries of (the great translator) Nubs (gnubs pa) onwards. On the Divisions of the Great Completion (rDzogs pa chen po kun byed) he received 'The Five First Translated Practices' (sna 'gyur lnga), 'The Thirteen Subsequently Translated Practices' (phyis 'gyur bcu gsum) and 'The Eighteen Divisions of the Mother and Son on the Mind Section' (sems sde ma bu bco brgyad).[11] He received the cycle of Klong sde and so forth. He also heard the 'General Tantra on the Bases' (zhi byed rgyud phyi ma) and the 'Termas' of Guru Rinpoche (guru'i gter ma). Furthermore, he received teachings on many treatises on the practice of medicine, on arts, on the practice of taking the essence (bcud len) and on healing (mkhyud spyad) and he became a scholar beyond measure in terms of their meaning.

Being not yet at ease, he exerted himself to acquire still more good qualities. He did not take a rest during the day and hardly slept at night, but exerted himself in the recitations of secret mantra and the meditation on the generation and completion stages and thereby he received visions of the Meditation Buddhas. He received the realization of stabilization of the generation stage and obtained the signs of touching and seeing.

He possessed such inconceivable powers that people often came to him instead of his grandfather with the request to subdue evil spirits and demons and so on. These non-humans would instantly offer up their lives to him, would respectfully bow down and would grant him the common powerful attainments and so on. In short, he became a great holder of mantra and of the vajra.

He also saw the necessity of taking ordination in the doctrine of Lord Buddha and intended, after receiving ordination, to keep up both the Dharma of transmissions (lung gi chos) through giving teachings and the Dharma of realization (rtogs pa'i chos) through the practice of meditation.

Then, in the year of the female fire sheep (1307), when he was 18 years old, he received the ordination ceremony (rab byung) from the abbot Rinchen Senge Pal Zangpo (rin chen seng ge dpal bzang po), who headed a lineage of learned translators and the novice vows (dge tshul) from the mighty scholar who was known as a person beautified by the perfect and continual practice of the three higher trainings called Tsadma'i kyebu (tshad ma'i skyes bu) also called Lobpon Rigna Thigpa and also called Sönam Gon (bsod nams mgon), who acted as the instructor.

Having received ordination he exerted himself to guard his moral discipline as carefully as he protected his eyes. Six times by day and night, he examined himself, whether there were any retributions of faults in his mental continuum or not. He studied and contemplated the 'Root Sutra of Vinaya' (mdo rtsa), 'The Vinaya Commentary' and 'The Concise Words of the Vows' and so on. Inbetween these he studied, with the same abbot, the methods to generate the mind of enlightenment and the Abhisamayalankara.

He then made the firm resolve to study (Haribhadra's) 'Short commentary on the Abhisamayalankara' (phar phyin 'grel chung) very hard for two years in order to gain a complete understanding free from doubts about this text and the meaning of this holy teaching at all costs, not caring whether he would die or suffer or not. He remained completely indifferent to food and clothing and all other hardships, and was pleased with anything he received. During the day he was so busy that he had no time to eat. When his garments were torn, he took no time to sew them. At night he did not even take time to sleep nor in the evening to fill the oil-lamps. At the break of day he would exert himself more in training his mind, until his body was the color of burnt meat and his forearms became like dry wood. He became very emaciated and thin and turned into an object of everyone's compassion. When the two years had passed he had mastered every word of the text and the explanations of the minor commentary, and he was able to correct it. He fully understood the meaning of the extensive, medium and short

'Perfection of Wisdom Sutras'.[12] On top of this he also became an expert in the commentaries on 'The Twenty Thousand verses' (nyi khri snang ba), the 'Commentary on the Eight Thousand Verses' (brgyad stong 'grel ba), (Asanga's) 'Yogacarya Bhumi' (sa sde lnga)[13] and (Asanga's) 'Two Compendiums': Abhidharmasamuccaya (chos mngön pa kun btus) and Mahayana sangraha (theg pa chen po bsdus pa); (Vasubandhu's) 'Eight Treatises' (prakarana sde brgyad)[14] and other texts and explained them. At the time of the new translations he wrote an extensive presentation on these.

While Buton combined his studies of 'Short Commentary on the Abhisamayalankara' with giving teachings, others who had studied with him had not reached such proficiency. Yet some exerted themselves right from the beginning to debate with him. Some people had studied quite well and doubted if he had a correct understanding of the meaning. Others said that Buton Rinpoche merely read the texts by putting them under his arm and some said that he just said something out of the blue and they doubted his realizations. Thus there was a lot of gossip about him. They then decided that they would check his teachings and attended his teachings in secret. Thus both scholars and fools went to his teachings to check his explanations thoroughly and they found that these were without any mistakes. He also explained the sources from the Indian commentaries. Listening to this they were all astounded. One person said that he possessed excellent wisdom and was pleasant and respectful. Another person said: "If one needs to have wisdom like Buton, I have to admit that I am a person who does not know much about the perfection of wisdom." And yet another person said: "Even though we have studied together, he knows everything and I don't. My lack of knowledge must be due to my teacher being partial," thus firmly indicting his teacher.

The spiritual teachers Rong Rigs, Ngag Cig, Zhang Yam and others, who lived in the temple of the Trophu Ganden Monastery, claimed to be masters in the meaning of the scriptural transmissions and logic, but in a discussion of the 'Abhisamayalankara' (phar phyin) and the Compendium (bsdus pa) they could not compete with Buton in terms of the meaning of the scriptural transmissions and of logic. He became even more famous than these teachers and was especially renowned throughout Tibet for his great wisdom. From this same teacher he heard the teachings on the Abhisamayalankara in the tradition of (the translator) Ngog (rnog blo ldan shes rab) many times. He also studied the Abhisamayalankara in the tradition of Drom (Brom ston pa) and in the tradition of Lu.

He read their commentaries and inbetween he studied the Sutra Pitaka, listening to teachings on Perfection of Wisdom such as 'The Twenty Thousand Verses' (nyi khri snang ba) and the 'Commentary on the Eight Thousand Verses' (brgyad stong 'grel ba) and on the 'Bodhisattvacaryavatara' and so on. He studied the Vinaya Pitaka, such as the 'Root Sutra of Vinaya' and the 'Continuum of the Flower Garland' (me tog phreng rgyud) and so on. He studied all the commentaries on valid cognition without exception such as the 'Compendium of Valid Cognition' (tshad ma kun las btus pa/ Pramanasamuccaya, by Acharya Dignaga) and so on. In particular, he listened many times to the main commentary on this, the 'Discernment of Valid Cognition' (tshad ma rnam par nges pa/ Pramanaviniscaya).

After he had finished the teachings on the Abhisamayalankara and on the Compendiums (bsdus pa) during the winter term of studies, from the beginning of the spring term he took up the text on the 'Discernment of Valid Cognition' until the beginning of the spring term of the following year. Thus during one year he mainly studied the 'Discernment of Valid Cognition'.

On top of that he studied thoroughly the 'Seven Treatises on Valid Cognition' (tshad ma sde bdun/sapta pramanashastra, by Dharmakirti) together with the 'Sutra on Valid Cognition' and completed that. He reached the state of a matchless unrivaled scholar, being completely unobscured about all the meanings of the words of the great commentaries on valid cognition, such as those of the Abbot Alankara, Acharya Dharmottana, Devendrabuddhi, Shakyabuddhi, Jnyana Shri and the others. His fame as a scholar pervaded everywhere on earth and by (his knowledge of the) scriptural transmissions and reasoning he defeated his serious opponents, including the members of the Bonpo school travelling around for their examinations, after which they embraced the correct views.

While walking on the mountain (chag pa dri gong gi shug pa ri) under the green juniper trees, he studied the 'Abhidharmasamuccaya' and mastered, every morning, seven sheets of arrow length of the original treatise and five sheets of its commentaries. In the evenings, primarily he would give teachings on these in a skilful way and thus within one month he became well versed in the meaning of the words of the 'Abhidharmasamuccaya' (chos mgnon pa kun btus, by Asanga).

Inbetween times he incidentally studied the 'Compendium of the Mahayana Vehicle' (theg chen bsdus) and the 'Five Great Stages' (sa sde lnga, by Asanga) and so on, and as he studied the 'Root Transmission of Vinaya' (lung ma mo), he became very well versed in the meaning of the words of the Three Pitakas.

He also studied the 'Root of Wisdom' (dbu ma rtsa ba shes rab/Mula-madhyamikakarika) and so on about Madhyamika philosophy and applied them very well in his mind, after which his fame as a scholar pervaded everywhere in Tibet.

While he studied the larger scriptures, he also concurrently studied Mahamudra (phyag chen brda'i skor) and the practice of Self-Healing (ngal gso) with Acharya Tshad ma'i Kyebu, and inbetween times he also listened to many teachings on the oral instructions (man ngag) such as on the 'One Hundred Instructions' (man ngag brgya rtsa).

From the great compassionate master Yang rtse ba Rinchen Senge, whose name was very well known and who was a great knowledge holder, he principally received the exposition of the empowerments of Chakrasamvara in the tradition of Ganthapada (dril bu pa) and the explanations of the Root Tantra and so on. He received the empowerments of the Great Bliss Goddess (bde chen ral cig ma/maha sukha ekatsati) and the explanations of these. He received empowerments of Yamantaka such as the Zhang tradition of Dra Nag (dgra nag) and the Kyo tradition of Bhairava. He received empowerment of the Great Wheel Vajrapani and explanations on Vajrapani.

He received the empowerment of Red Tara and so on about Tara and the blessings of the Two-Faced and so on about (Vajra) Varahi. He received the Nine Crowns of Kun Rig (kun rig gtsug dgu) and so on about Yoga and the White Vidarana (rnam 'joms dkar po) and so on about Vidarana; the Sound of the Drum of Immortality and so on about Amitayus ('chi med rnga sgra); the Poems on the Resource and so on about the Six Yogas of Naropa (thabs lam tshigs bcad ma sogs na ro chos drug gi skor); the 13 Explanations and so on about Mahamudra (brda rtsa bcu gsum) as well as various other profound oral instructions such as the Various Deep Upadeshas (zhi cod rin spungs), the Excellent Praise of the Qualities of Wisdom and so on, praises and sadhanas of Manjushri; the 'One Hundred Sadhanas' and so on of the Great Compassionate One (Avalokiteshvara), the oral instructions on the practice of the six perfections and others besides.

He studied the 'Beneath the Earth' (sa 'og) and the 'Supreme Dance' (gar mchog) practice of Vaisravana (rnam sras/Vaisravana), as well as the 'Secret Lineage' and the 'Six Sky Goers' (mkha 'gro drug) and so on of Mahakala (mgon po), and became well versed in these. Furthermore, he studied an incredible number of empowerments, explanations, blessings and transmissions and received limitless teachings and instructions and followed the instructions as they were taught.

With the Master Namnangba Yonten Gyatso (rnam snang ba yon tan rgya mtsho) he studied the 'Opening the Door to the Practice of Chöd (gcod yul nam mkha' sgo 'byed) and the 'Instructions on the Sun Above' (gdams pa nyi gros ma'i gong khug) and so on. With Acharya Dondrub Pal (slob dpon don grub pal), elder brother of the Master Jangchub Pal (bla ma byang chub dpal), he principally studied Hayagriva in the Ngog (rngog) tradition and the root text and commentary of the Shikshasamuccaya (bslab btus rtsa 'grel). Also, inbetween times, he studied the Abhisamayalankara (phar phyin).

From his father, the glorious Master Trag Tön Gyaltsen (brag ston rgyal mtshan), he received the great 'Vajra Beneath the Earth' (rdo rje sa og) and so on about the 'Good Dakinis of Vajrapani' (phyag rdor 'gro bzang ma), and inbetween times he studied the 'Discernment of Valid Cognitions' and the 'Compendium'. He also listened to many separate instructions with the Sage Togdan Sörin (rtogs ldan bsod rnam rin chen). With Konchog Zhonnu (dkon mchog gzhon nu), the fourth successor of the great abbots of the Trangmo (grang mo) transmission, he studied mainly Avalokiteshvara in the Kadampa tradition (don zhags bha' gdams lugs) as well as other practices concurrently.

With the Master Jamkya Namkha Pal ('jam skya nam mkha dpal) he studied mainly several explanations of the Sakya tradition on the 'Commentary on the Compendium on Valid Cognition' (tshad ma rnam 'grel, by Dharmakirti) and inbetween he studied the Mahamaya and so on. With the great Master Tishi Kunlo (ti shi kun blo) he principally studied the mind of enlightenment according to the Madhyamika tradition and he did various other practices as well.

In short, he studied some of the most distinguished teachings and gained a thorough understanding of these. He correctly applied himself to their practice by means of his impeccable behavior and became a very noble person. He was an expert in teaching, debating and writing and accomplished simultaneously hearing, contemplating and meditating in one sitting. Whatever texts he undertook to study for his own sake and for the sake of others, he could do so and he would complete them accordingly. He gave a great deal of thought to accomplishing the purpose of others like a father of all transmigrating beings. He made the firm resolve: "May I completely master all the practices of Lord Buddha's doctrine, both of dialectics and of tantra." And he thought: "May I never get tired of listening to or teaching the root of the doctrine."

After one year had passed since he commenced his studies on the texts on Valid Cognition, in the springtime he went for a course of study and debate to the central country with his father Trag Tönpa, and that summer they went to attend a large seminar at Tsang (gtsang). At that time numerous famous scholar monks from central Tibet (dbus) such as the younger Jang Zhon Shag Zhongpa (byang gzhon shag gzhong pa) and Tsan Gonpa (rtsan dgon pa) and so on from Kharag, and Palden Senge, U Tsepa, Jamkya (dpal ldan seng ge, dbu tshad pa, 'jam skya) and so on from Tsang, who considered themselves to be great scholars, were to attend. The word was spread around that Buton Khache of Throphu would come to the seminar and that they must be attentive as he had superb wisdom which was not easy to compete with. In short, he was able to have the capacity to liberate by reasoning and to eliminate any number of doubts by his virtues. Because he had perfected an ocean of philosophical tenets, he was fearless in refutation. In fact he had become a great scholar, well versed in the presentations of practices and non-practices by applying the power of the wisdom of ultimate and relative reality.

When he was only 21 years old, he refuted all controversies of wrong views completely, and defeated and uprooted them completely with scriptural transmissions and reasoning. Because nobody could compete with him, they humbly held their heads bent down. Through this debate all came to hold the non-mistaken view and he brought them to a conducive direction. All unanimously agreed that this teacher possessed the right Dharma language and he became even more glorious.

Next (he thought that), in order to ripen others, one first needs to ripen oneself and that he was not completely perfect in terms of the Doctrine, despite his striving. He thought that if one does not take full ordination, one is like children who can't see clearly because of the tears in their eyes. To engage in the doctrine without being fully ordained as a bhikshu, one is not able to enact the Vinaya practices for individual liberation and does not have authority over the rituals of Vinaya. If one does not have this, one is not fit to be a teacher who gives empowerments and teaches the tradition of secret mantra. Seeing that the bhikshus are praised as the best of all teachers in the excellent traditions of secret mantra, the Master of the Dharma decided to request full ordination.

In the year of the male water bird, when he was 23 years old, the Lord of Dharma took ordination in the eastern residence of the market town of Tsang called Tshon 'dus 'gur mo, from the great abbot, the gloriously good Tragpa Zhonnu Pal Zangpo (gzhon nu dpal bzang po) who was the fourth in the lineage of the Panchen Abbots and one of the famous 16 Arhats, with the great bodhisattva Sonam Trag (bsod nams grags) acting as the Acharya and the great holder of monastic discipline Sonam Zangpo (bsod nams bzang po) acting as the secret preceptor. The ordination took place in the midst of a gathering of 22 people, with the great holder of the classes of the Sangha of faith Konchog Zangpo (dkon mchog bzang po) acting as the leader.

People from various regions assembled there and many businessmen came and thus a great marketplace appeared around the lamas' household. Buton Rinpoche was given full ordination, through which he adopted the aspect of a great Arhat. With this abbot he mainly studied the Pratimoksha Sutra and so on, and he also studied Ushnishavijaya (gtsug tor rnam rgyal), the Heart of Wisdom Sutra and the Sutra Practices (mdo sgrub) and so on.

From his preceptor, the great bodhisattva Sonam Tragpa, he mainly received an 'Explanation on the Application of the Commentary to the Root Text of the Vinaya Sutra' and he studied the 'Concise Words of the Vows' and explanations on the 'Pratimoksha Sutra' and (Gunaprabha's) 'One Root of a Hundred Actions' (las brgya rtsa gcig) and so on.

Furthermore, he generated the wishing mind of enlightenment and the engaging mind of enlightenment, besides which he studied the 'Thought Training of Avalokiteshvara' (don zhags blo sbyong) etc. When he studied the Thought Training he particularly generated the pure urge for liberation and the precious mind of enlightenment. Furthermore, he exerted himself in recommending the urge for liberation and the mind of enlightenment. "Oh, now," he proclaimed, "Will death not come to you? I am ageing myself and I do not have long to go before I die." Saying these things he also turned others towards the urge for liberation.

When he heard the story of an evil person called Gonpo Dar, who killed his father with a bow and arrow, he spontaneously shed tears. In fact, there were many such instances of his realization of the urge for liberation and of love and compassion, but I have not written them all down because I fear (this biography) would become too long. Next he extensively listened to explanations at Thro phu with the armor of great perseverance. To fill himself still further with the Dharma, he mainly engaged in teachings of the 'Abhisamayalankara', 'Pramanavartika' and 'Collected Topics on Valid Cognition' and on the 'Abhidharmasamuccaya' by teaching them to others. Inbetween times he gave teachings several times at Khren Trag Lung ('khran brag lung), at Nyangro Shugpa Ri (nyang ro shug pa ri), at Tro Zang Kha (khro zangs kha) and at Latö Tekyu (la stod lte skyus) and other places, explaining the 'Abhisamayalankara', 'Abhidharmasamuccaya', 'Pramanavartika' and the 'Discernment of Valid Cognition' (Vinishcaya) and so on.

When he recited the 'Rituals of Vinaya' many times to memorize them, someone said: "His understanding may be great, but to whom has he given the vows of a bhikshu?" The same year when he memorized the 'Rituals of Vinaya' nine people came to him from Tö (stod) and requested him to grant them full ordination and he promised to act as their Acharya. In short, he acted as an abbot and as an Acharya to tens of thousands of bhikshus, sramaneras, ordained ones, holders of the vows for laypeople, etc.

In the daytime he studied untiringly and at night he steadily integrated the profound meditations on the practices of the yoga with signs and without signs[15] inseparably. He fully accomplished the meditations and recitations of the generation and completion stages of Chakrasamvara and the Great Wheel Vajrapani and so on, and when he finished the mantra recitations, he actually saw these Meditation Buddhas.

He exerted himself in the profound instructions on the 'Six Yogas of Naropa'[16] and the 'Instructions for Making One's Mind at Ease' (ngal gso). He also exerted himself in the meditations of the yoga without signs, such as the Datsa Zhichö Rinpung (brda rtsa zhi spyod rin spungs). Seeing his sincere way of life, his sponsors generated strong faith and a fervent regard and provided him with the necessary conducive conditions. Buton said: "If one has the capacity to (practice the) Dharma, one does not need to worry about conducive conditions. As we studied well, the sponsors have strong confidence and will provide us with abundant conducive conditions all the time."

When he taught the Dharma at Trophu (khro phu), there was a monk called Yeshe Senge who listened to the Abhisamayalankara; one day he was not present. Some days later he attended again. In the mind of the Lord of Dharma the thought arose: "Although I wish to work for the purpose of all sentient beings, I cannot even fulfil even the purpose of this single being." And he thought: "Up to now I have practiced as if I were a nobleman, but maybe I need to train myself more in order to work for the purpose of others."

Afterwards he associated with Chos rgyal and Zhang Yam and together they decided to go to the translator called Khenchen Tharpa Lotsawa, who was known in west, east and central India as the most famous and venerable scholar of Tibet and an authority on the oral instructions, and who had become a translator who was the eye of the world. They decided to request him for instruction in the Sanskrit language and in the six limbs of applying the advice on how to become a Buddha in one lifetime with one body. He put on a hat with a long point and a long flat topside, took one small book and went across the plains of Tagla Og. Between the places Layon and Dangkar he was greeted by some children who were playing and joyfully shouted, "Oh look, there's a pandit." They briefly halted in front of him and said, "Pandita, pandita, please say Namo Buddhaya." He considered this sound of children's voices to be a good sign.

When he arrived at Tharpa Ling he stayed in the company of this great translator for 14 months without interruption. In addition, he met with him for periods of about two, three or four months at a time. He studied thoroughly for more than four years altogether, principally the 'Sutra of the Tsandra Language', (sgra tsandra pa'o mdo) and its commentary and concurrently he trained in the 'Sutra of the Kalapa Language' and its commentary. He learnt Sanskrit, the language of the gods, including the 'Sutra' (mdo), the 'Dhatu' (byings), the 'Upasarga' (nye bsgyur), the nominal and verbal suffixes (su dang ti), the 'Unati', the Bidi Utpada, the Amarakosha and other texts, and studied them very well with their commentaries. Although there were many different alphabets in India, in the east, the west, Kashmir, Shri Lanka, Sindh and on the ocean shores, he understood many of them without having to learn how to read them. Exerting himself day and night in his practice and training, he became a very great translator without equal up to the present day.

Next he intended to request the (most) 'Precious Teachings' (gsung ngag rin po che). He offered a precious golden mandala to the Master Khenchen Lotsawa with the request to grant him the profound instructions on becoming a Buddha within one lifetime with a single body, the instruction of the six limbs (sbyor ba yan lag drug gi gdams pa).[17] The Master said: "You are a great holder of the Tripitaka with a good heart. You are a special recipient, who is energetic in actions and respectful in attitude. You are a great Master of the Dharma, who will serve as a great trunk of the secret mantra. Therefore I will confer the highest empowerment of Shri Kalachakra on you."

When the meaning of the empowerment was explained, he generated many doors of single-pointed concentration in his mind. He retreated in solitary meditation, staying in a cave of which the entrance was closed with clay, and achieved the power of the Rupakaya of appearance from within emptiness.

He developed various insights, such as the non-existence of the external and internal, the non-existence of above and below, the non-existence of in front and behind, the non-existence of prior and after, non-compounded phenomena, non-expression of time, non-partiality, the non-inherent existence of appearances, the non-grasping for the clear as real, true happiness without defilements, the splendor of the clear light, the non-inherent production of (the essential) nature, and the non-duality of relative and ultimate reality.

He saw the play of supporting and supported mandalas that arise from the spontaneous wisdom which is self-born and non-material and he saw the undefiled gods and goddesses, the heroes and heroines in the state of great bliss. He saw all external and internal phenomena as appearances of the mind. In the appearance of various minds he realized the emptiness of birth, abiding and cessation, and he realized the nature of emptiness as clear light. He also realized the essential points of bliss and emptiness and came to see everything as the play of Dharmakaya. He had a direct bare perception of the mode of existence of the channels, subtle energies and drops. He completed the skill of the great wisdom realizing the purity of the ultimate existence of subject and object.

He realized that all the wisdom that arose from the meditative concentration on the clear light was transcended in the mind at the time of its appearance, when its own clarity and light give way to the unborn great bliss whose nature is self-born and self-arisen. He generated all the single-pointed concentrations such as the precious luminosity (rin chen snang ba), the precious lamp (rin chen sgron ma), the moonlight (zla ba snang ba), and the sun lamp (nyi ma sgron ma) as well as the single-pointed concentration which sees all aspects (rnam pa thams cad gzigs pa) etc. He manifested endless realizations (nyams rtogs), clear visions (mthong snang), clairvoyance (mngon shes) and signs of accomplishment (grub rtags), but it is impossible to record them all as they are most uncommon.

He always thought of his master Khenchen Tharpa Lotsawa as a real Buddha and did not even for a moment consider him to be an ordinary person. He generally performed religious services to all his masters, but when he performed religious services (dus mchod) to this master he especially performed the Shri Kalachakra self-initiation and made extensive offerings of ritual cakes to the worldly ghosts and Dharma Protectors. He also made abundant and excellent food offerings to the Spiritual Community. Above all, he performed inwardly elaborate offerings of single-pointed concentration (nang ting nge 'dzin gyi mchod pa rgya chen po).

With this master he further studied all the famous tantras such as the 'Six Preparations' (sbyor ba drug) of Anupamarakshita (dpe med mtsho) about the six preparations; the 'Final Tantra' (rgyud phyi ma) etc. about Kalachakra; the 'Vajra Essence Commentary' (rdo rje snying 'grel); the 'Great Commentary of Naropa' (na' ro 'grel chen); the 'Completely Seizing the Good' (bzang po yongs bzung) etc. about Hevajra (kye rdor); 'Vajradaka' (rdo rje mkha 'gro) and the 'Commentary on the Praises to Vajrapani' and so on about Chakrasamvara (bde mchog); the 'Tantra of the Four Asanas' etc. on the four asanas; the 'Thirteen Red Messengers' and so on about Yamantaka; the Highest Yoga Tantra aspect of Miyowa and the sadhanas of the white and red Sarasvati (dbyangs can ma) and so on. He also extensively studied philosophy such as the 'Moonrays on the Essential Points' (gnad kyi zla zer) as well as poetry and metrical science (snyen dngags sdeb sbyor).

In the presence of the holy Master Palden Senge (dpal ldan seng ge) who was very famous and considered to be inseparable from Buddha Vajradhara, he combined the empowerments of Shri Kalachakra of the translator Ra Lotsawa and the translator Bromi Lotsawa and requested the performance of the practice mainly in the tradition of Ra Lotsawa. At the time of making that request, he saw that master change into Dorje Shug (rdo rje shugs). He studied all about Kalachakra and after that received the Lingma (gling ma) and so on about Hevajra. He also studied the 'Investigation of the Mind' (sems thag bcad pa) and so on about the paths; Ganthapada (dril bu pa) etc. about Chakrasamvara; the 'Manifestation of Vajravarahi' (phag mo mngon 'byung) and so on about Vajravarahi; the 'Yoga of the Power of Space' (rnal 'byor nam mkha'i dbang) etc.; and the 'Four Asanas' (gdan gzhi), Mahamaya and the Tantra of Buddhakapala (sangs rgyas thod pa). He received the 'Uddiyana Tara' (o rgyan sgrol ma) and so on about Tara; the traditions of Phag ('phags) and Yeshe Zhab (ye shes zhab) about Guhyasamaja (gsang 'dus); the 'Red Bhairava Yamantaka' ('jigs byed gzhed dmar) and so on about Yamantaka; the 'Great Wheel' ('khor chen) and so on about Vajrapani; the 'Vajradhatu' (rdo rje dbyings) and so on about Yoga; and the 'Manifestation of Vairocana' (rnam snang mngon byung) and so on, all in the class of Charya Tantra. He received the empowerments for some of these while for others he received the explanations (of the practice) and for others the oral instructions together with the implements. In addition, he received empowerment in the 'Protecting Lord of the World' (rigs gi 'jig rten mgon po) and Highest Yoga Tantra aspect of Miyowa.

He received the empowerment of Vajramala (rdo rje phreng ba) and so on and subsequent permission to practice Ushnishavijaya (gtsug tor rnam rgyal ma). He also studied many sutras such as the 'Sutra at the Request of Samantabhadra'. Inbetween receiving these teachings in this way, he gave teachings principally on the Abhisamayalankara and also on the 'Discernment of the Aspects' and on the 'Abhidharmasamuccaya'.

Served by his disciples Senge Yeshe Pal (seng ge ye shes dpal) and Dargya (dar rgyas), he composed a commentary which was the 'Brief Commentary on the Abhisamayalankara' (phar phyin 'grel chung). In addition, he composed a 'General History of Buddhism' (bstan pa sbyi'i chos 'byung); a 'Sadhana of the Great Dharma Protectors' (chos skyong chen po'i sgrub thabs); the 'Period of Emptiness on the Path of Seeing' (mthong lam stong thun); the "Elimination of Incorrect Views' (lta ba ngan sel) and the 'Time Element in the Vinaya Tradition' ('dul ba'i lugs kyi dus); a 'Praise to the Great Wheel Vajrapani' ('khor chen gyi stod pa) etc.

After this he intended to train his mind further in the Shri Kalachakra practice and he went to Rong with Lama Yeshe Pal. Since Lama Sherab Senge had passed away, he went to the regent called Dorje Gyaltsen Pal Zangpo (rdo rje rgyal mtshan dpal bzang po), who was very well versed in philosophy as well as in the tantras and had unrivalled knowledge of the meaning and the words of the Kalachakra Tantra. He heard the complete teachings on Kalachakra, combining the opinions of Ra Lotsawa and Bromi Lotsawa in a special manner of explanation of all of their individual points. He possessed the oral instructions of all the important points of the practice as well as all the implements of Kalachakra without exception. The Lama said: "Oh, I recognize in thee a Lord of the Dharma. Now may all have a happy frame of mind."

The two Lords of Dharma stayed together without interruption for nine months. They went through all the explanations twice and indicated all the special points. He also made notes on the difficult parts (zin bris), made drawings (sa ris), questions (dri gtugs), careful considerations (bsam mno) and exerted himself even more. Thus he became an unrivalled scholar in the meaning and the words of the tantras and commentaries of Shri Kalachakra. Even at that time (Buton) listened to explanations and gave teachings on the Abhisamayalankara. On top of being well versed in the field of philosophy and a master of all the great classes of tantra in secret mantra, he perfected himself as a scholar of the Kalachakra tantra. Thus he became like a brilliant sun mandala in the sky amidst the mere starlike scholars who were holders of either the teachings on philosophy or tantra and many scholars no longer even dared to speak in his presence.

He always valued Kalachakra highly and when he gave teachings he considered that to be the action of Shri Kalachakra. He considered the mandala rituals from the Kalachakra Tantra to be more difficult than those of the other tantras and the protection circle of Kalachakra to be amazing compared to the mandala rituals of other tantras. "A practice like this does not exist easily. Would you please come here, students?" he would say and he would make drawings of the mandala for the students at the side of the Dharma throne. He also wrote a 'Small Text to Not Forget' (brjad don dpe chung) and the 'Essential Points of the Magic Circle' ('phrul 'khor gyi gnad) and so on according to the Kalachakra tantra and its commentaries, and he continued to perform his practices.

When asked about the essential points that are difficult to learn he would never become irritated with certain questions as other Geshes would. When asked a question he would smile and with love he would reply fully, giving the sense of the words and gently providing an appropriate answer without any mistake in the order. Thus he was always able to continue to speak at ease saying, "It is like this..." and then give repeated clarifications.

"When you study such a stainless Dharma practice you should ask questions. In particular, as we all are tantrikas, if we do not get to ask questions about the subtle parts of the practice we will not become good teachers," he said and, jokingly, "Probably you are all scholars around here, since no one is asking me questions. Because it is difficult to have instant results, it takes earnest application, and if there is something uncomfortable then please ask me.

"Lord Buddha taught the profound and vast Dharma practices which were garnered by the collectors of the teaching, explained by the great scholars and siddhas, translated by the translators and pandit scholars and arranged by scholars, and thus the tradition of explanation has remained continuous, the stream of empowerments has remained unbroken, adulterations have been avoided, the teachings have not been mixed up, the words of honor have not degenerated, the continuity of the Mahasiddhas of the oral tradition of the words of Lord Buddha (bka' brgyud grub thob) has remained unbroken and the power of the blessings has not diminished. The profound sutra and tantra commentaries, which are like an ointment for the eyes, have been put into practice. We should apply ourselves in this way to listening to Dharma teachings about the general paths of all the Buddhas and Bodhisattvas and thus acquire an inexhaustible collection of merit. Let us not waste it but use it for the vast purpose of self and others," he would say earnestly.

With the great Master Dorje Gyaltsen Pal Zangpo he further studied the tantras such as 'Three Wheels of the Black Yamantaka' (nag 'jigs) and the 'Root Tantra of Manjushri; sadhanas such as the 'Ocean of Sadhanas' (sgrub thabs rgya mtsho), and others besides.

He received instructions transmitted from the great lord of yogis Vibutipada, who was himself a direct disciple of the Mahasiddha Jalandharipa on 'Lighting the Tummo' (gtum mo 'bar 'dzag), the 'Seven Emanated Circles to Overcome Hindrances' (gegs sel 'khrul 'khor bdun pa) and the '(Method) to Take the Essence from Milk' ('o ma'i bcud len) as well as many other instructions.

Inbetween these he received oral instructions of the Kadampa lineage from the venerable scholar Kumara Siddhi, who was a direct disciple of the Master Jam Lingpa (byams gling pa) from Phar Phug Rong (bar phug rong) and lived near Yongru Kokha (yong ru ko kha). While doing so he practiced the instructions he received from these masters and increased his qualities.

At that time the great master Dragpa Gyaltsen (grags pa rgyal mtshan), who belonged to the lineage of the ancient traditions of Tse Cidrug (lce phyi 'brug) and of Jnanasiddhi and so on had sincere respect for the doctrine and was a great sponsor of offerings. He also was considered to be an emanation of the Great King Vaishravana (rnam thos sras) and was repairing the temple of which he was the master, situated in the northern valley of Khabacan (kha ba can), in the midst of glorious snow mountains. This temple had been built by the great Cetsun Sherab Jungnä (lce btsun shes rab 'byung gnas) who was a direct disciple of Lama Dorje Danpa (bla ma rdo rje gdan pa) at the place where a statue of Avalokiteshvara had miraculously appeared and where Atisha (Dipamkara Shri Jnana) had performed an invocation ritual (rab gnas). The temple was called Zhalu Serkhang.[18]

He hauled a famous species of wood from the region called Lhomon and employed well-trained craftsmen from the region of China east of Tibet (Shargya). The temple had a triple pagoda roof made of turquoise-colored tiles surmounted by big golden domes. It had turquoise-colored balcony railings with inlaid works of patterned squares adorned with golden domes. The golden building (serkhang) had a pagoda roof of three layers. The other buildings had a pagoda roof of two layers. All of these were decorated with golden nets with small and large ornamental bells. Inside there were marvellous images of the Tathagatas in 101 different sparkling colors. In one of the twin chapels towards the west, the main image was the Avalokiteshvara which had miraculously appeared and in the other chapel the main image was one of Vairocana. In the southern chapels the chief images were the Buddhas of the three times, while in the northern chapel the chief image was Shakyamuni Buddha. In the chapel to the east the main image was of the Great Mother (Prajnaparamita). Beneath those there was the protector shrine of the Great King Vaishravana (rnam thos sras), surrounded by his countless assistants; all of these made from precious jewels.

There was also a collection of the great scriptures with the teachings of Lord Budda (bka' 'gyur) and so on written in pure gold. In front of them all were perfectly arranged offerings of precious materials. Outside there was a huge metal fence all around, within which houses were built with rooms that were offered to each of the resident Sangha-members. He also established the four great offerings which take place in the first month of each season, offerings to the Three Jewels and offerings of income to the Sangha-members. Thus there was a lot of support for the resident Sangha and he maintained his many subjects in accordance with the rules of the holy Dharma and the four methods for ripening others.

In short, Dragpa Gyaltsen practiced just like the precious Dharma kings of the past, the Bodhisattvas Trisong Detsen (khri srong lde btsan) and Tri Ralpacan (khri ral pa can), etc. With this temple the friend of the doctrine intended to make the general doctrine of Lord Buddha flourish and especially to spread the Mahayana teachings, to make all the monks have good health and sufficient sponsorship and to cause all sentient beings of the kingdom to have happiness. Thus the temple was rebuilt and it became as beautiful as can be imagined. This fulfillment, he thought, is all due to the blessing of the Three Jewels. Then he realized that there was only a small number of Sangha-members in his temple and he wished sincerely to have a Sangha community as vast as an ocean and to have a Dharma leader who combined the qualities of learning, nobility and seriousness (mkhas btsun bzang) as well as 100 spiritual friends who explain the Dharma. Thinking this, he decided to dedicate himself to finding a good Dharma teacher and he requested the Buddhas to prophesy who would be suitable.

He placed many offerings for the Three Jewels, performed service to the Sangha community, offered ritual cakes to the Dharma Protectors and generated regard for the names of all the native and foreign spiritual teachers that were known as scholars, venerable and good teachers; he repeated their names and observed his dreams. By the power of his pure extraordinary resolve (lhag bsam) the Buddhas prophesied in his dream that a Lord of Dharma and great translator would come there and the general doctrine would flourish and spread, and in particular the teachings of the Mahayana scriptures would flourish and spread even further and would be understood correctly.

He then sent a letter of request to the abbot and teacher, the students and Sangha community residing in Throphu and to the Lord of Dharma, inviting him to come to Zhalu.[19] Most of the people involved, including the disciple Lozang, said that it was not good to go, while others including Yeshe Pal gave their consent. While his students disagreed, Buton Rinpoche decided to check for himself. He saw that there was a relation between himself and the sponsor from a previous prayer and that it would be beneficial for the doctrine and the Pitakas and that, although there would be some initial difficulties in subduing them, in the long run it would prove to be beneficial for many transmigrating beings. Thus he (Buton) accepted the invitation to go to Zhalu.

In the year of the male iron monkey (1320), when he was 31 years old, Buton Rinpoche arrived in Zhalu. Just as previously the sponsor Anathapindada (mgon med zas byin) had offered food to the Buddha, this great sponsor generated great respect for the Lord of Dharma and rendered him proper service. He offered his body, possessions, family and servants and after that made requests for the spread of the doctrine of Lord Buddha in general and for the flourishing and increase of the Sangha community in particular.

He invited (Buton) with great faith, served him with a lot of respect and worshipped him in many ways. (Treating Buton) like his crown jewel he made manifold offerings. With great joy he made offerings to the spiritual master at his enthronement. Buton Rinpoche studied the Nyal Tig (gnyal tig) with the teacher and chanting master Tashi Zangpo (bkra shis bzang po) and the Tig Chung (tig chung) with Buton Senge Öd (bu ston seng ge 'od). After that he started a program there which included the Commentary on the Abhisamayalankara that he himself had composed along with Nyalpa's commentary and the 'Discernment of Valid Cognition', the 'Abhidharmasamuccaya' and the 'Vinaya Root Sutra'.

At that time Buton Rinpoche's great fame had spread everywhere but he wished to further expand his work for the benefit of transmigrating beings. The evil spirits and nagas were disturbed by jealousy and turned against him, through which the mind of some people was changed. Some no longer respected his Dharma discourses and behaved rebelliously. He thought: "Indeed I am their teacher who explains the Dharma, but in terms of commitment some students behave like people who argue about wealth and have a lot of criticism. Though I am their teacher some do not accept me in their mind and try to expel me like soldiers who throw stones at a crazed dog. When they meet a person with good qualities, they try from all sides to oust him like a huge stone from the field. While I give them good advice with the motivation to benefit others, they react as enemies, like a son whose father was killed. Even though they cannot stand by themselves, they criticize others and their criticism is like the recital of mantras to cure leprosy going on day and night. They are like childish beings who lie in ambush waiting to hear word of the three: greed, hatred and ignorance. When they hear a discourse on the Dharma, they behave like people who beat an old donkey until it becomes completely debilitated. In such circumstances it would not be correct to be the object of others' enmity while giving Dharma teachings. There is a danger that the bed of Dharma would become a very ordinary matter. They are proud to know the words whereas they do not understand their meaning. As they do not liberate their own mental continuum, what will happen when they give teachings to others?

In his meditation he thought: "I have practiced what is difficult and carried the burden of the great vehicle and developed manifold good qualities which I brought to perfection. Although I wear the great armor of benefiting the doctrine and all sentient beings, the purpose of sentient beings is hindered by unfortunate conditions which are the result of some previously collected evil karma." Thus he examined the validity of the teachings on the interdependent relations between past actions and their results, such as the pain caused by a sandalwood splinter in Lord Buddha's foot.

For a while he thought about a method to tame all beings to be subdued, and decided to talk with the great sponsor Dragpa Gyaltsen. He said: "You who possess wealth with a thousandfold splendor and great fame, which originated from the huge store of your previously collected merit, great sponsor, whose kingdom has victory banners that extend to the four continents, you who have perfect faith in the doctrine, please listen to me.

"This precious lamp, the doctrine of Lord Buddha, depends on the teachings of a pure urge for liberation. When both theory and practice become excellent, well-being and happiness come forth for oneself and others. To benefit the doctrine in this way, we need conducive conditions to organize Dharma teachings. We also need teachers endowed with moral discipline and exceptional qualities, great enthusiasm, many transmissions, skilled in speech and loving in nature, without laziness, who possess both the doctrine as well as patience and skilful methods as well as pure followers. We need obedient students, who have the mind of a caretaker, who respect Lord Buddha, the doctrine and the spiritual teachers, and who have given up the three faults of the wrong recipient: the vessel upside down, the leaking and the polluted vessel.

The general motivation of the teacher and students should be concordant and both the spiritual and material conducive conditions need to coincide. There should be no interferences by humans and non-humans and it is very important that the mind is absorbed into the Dharma. If this is not established, the fault arises of bad teachers who do not consider moral discipline to be the heart of the doctrine and therefore will not experience its ripening result in the definite goodness of a higher rebirth as a god or a human and in liberation. In their shameless state they are like empty ears of corn. If one does not mix one's own continuum with the Dharma, one is like a talking parrot when one teaches it to others.

"Even if the teacher is good by nature, if connected to bad students he is like a sandalwood tree with venomous snakes coiled around it. Relying only on himself, his qualities do not increase and as he guards his jealousy and hatred towards those who do have qualities, he also severs the continuum of the qualities of other students. He is like a barren woman. In short, bad teachers and bad students disturbed by human and non-human interferences work adversely on the teachings. They do not benefit the doctrine and are causes for people to wander in cyclic existence.

"I was born here in Tibet amidst the ranges of snow mountains where, due to the power of evil karma collected in previous lives, the real Dharma declines and false Dharma flourishes. The land is inhabited by people who throw away those practicing Dharma like grass. People here give up the life of Dharma for food and guard their moral discipline in a hypocritical manner. They practice studying teachings and contemplating merely for fame in this life. When they are capable of doing something on their own, they are haughty with pride and compare themselves with everyone. They accomplish little, are restless and criticize anyone who acts in accordance with the Dharma. They do not act in accordance with the Dharma, yet wonder why they experience painful ripening results. I do not know what behavior pleases everyone.

"Whatever I undertake is held to be a fault. What is the use of giving teachings when there is no benefit for me and only harm for others? What should I do as a teacher in this situation, when whatever I do in terms of eating, sitting, going or walking becomes the cause of other people's anger? In this way my life will not last long, my sense organs will become unclear and the suffering of birth and death is extremely hard to bear. I think the time has come to practice what little knowledge I have."

After (Buton) had thus spoken, he took a rest for a while. Then the great landlord Dragpa Gyaltsen, who was a constant sponsor of the Dharma and had great respect for the Dharma and his daughter Dzom Bum, together with all the sponsors and their retinue and the virtuous monks and the students were very surprised and assembled in front of Buton Rinpoche. The ones that had misbehaved were all scrutinized and, their faults being pointed out to them, all the harmful students were made to feel ashamed and repentant. With their heads humbly bent, they unanimously requested Buton Rinpoche to turn the Wheel of Dharma, just like Brahma and Indra had requested Lord Buddha to turn the Wheel of Dharma.

They said: "Great all-knowing abbot, you are the only eye of transmigrating beings. We request you to stay at ease in this place and to turn the Wheel of Dharma extensively. We shall practice exactly according to your explanations. We feel ashamed and repent of everything we have done wrong. Please do not allow these mistakes to become obscurations for us, but stay with us."

After this request the great master Buton considered that it was not correct to neglect them by remaining indifferent as they showed sincere interest in the Dharma and reverentially paid their respect and the time had come to cultivate them.

He said: "In general, no matter how much one helps sentient beings of this degenerate era, they harm oneself in return. This is the nature of childish beings. I promise, however, that I will take care of you both spiritually and materially. Although I was focused on the doctrine and the Sangha, great harm had befallen me posing danger to my life, but it would be shameless and inconsiderate if I were to ignore the words of the great sponsor. There would not be a clear reason and it would become the cause of ill-repute and then what could we do? In many respects it would not be correct. It is also not proper if the monastery has a lot of disturbances because of greed and hatred. By following this greed and hatred the Sangha, the sponsor and the lineage of the doctrine would be harmed. This is not good. As all of you are very firm in your requests, I will stay for a while and give some Dharma teachings."

He started comprehensive explanations on mantra and dialectics and established a great school. While internally he remained absorbed in the profound single-pointed concentration which does not discriminate between different aspects (mi rtog pa'i ting nge dzin), externally he was tireless in giving Dharma teachings, debate and in the composition of books. In the company of the Mahasiddha Ze Marpa he mainly studied the empowerments in the Luipa tradition of Heruka and of the 'Thirteen Red Yamantakas' (gshes dmar bcu gsum pa) and so on. Inbetween he studied Chakrasamvara etc.

Formerly the great master Atisha had resided at Zhalu Riphug and a lot of clay tablets of his meditation Buddha were made and put into a small hollow construction with a small stupa on top. He took this as a basis and erected a great temple there along with accommodation for the Sangha community.

Previously when Buton Rinpoche studied Kalachakra with the great master Rongpo they had a discussion and Buton had asked for someone with knowledge of Guhyasamaja. The master had said: "Well then, I have a Dharma-brother Acharya Arya (slob dpon 'phags pa) who is a perfect scholar on the subject of Guhyasamaja. Not only that, he is also an extremely good scholar of Yoga. He has knowledge beyond description and holds extensive transmissions on these subjects." When searching for this scholar Acharya Arya he had difficulties finding him. Because of the similarity of names he mistook the name for someone else. In passing he had heard of an Acharya Arya who was learned but had violated his vows and, without further examination, he had felt disgusted and turned away.

Later he heard that the master was living in Kyi Khor (skyi 'khor) and he sent Geshe Sonam Rinchen to him as a messenger to invite him to Riphug and request teachings. Then he was suddenly given a vase filled to the brim with water by a woman, and a vajra and a bell by a yogi who appeared and said: "Previously these were yours." Pleased by this he invited the master, intending to study mainly the Guhyasamaja Tantra, but Acharya Arya said: "You are not a person who needs a word-by-word explanation. You only need an explanation of the difficult points and the rest you can read directly." The Lord of Dharma then spoke: "This is not sufficient for me; please explain the teaching to me in detail."

Saying that he must then first carry out the practical instructions of the 'Five Preparations', the master and student retired into solitary meditation. At the time when the empowerment and teachings were conferred he entered the single-pointed concentration which understands the object of prayers, and Buton Rinpoche saw many Buddhas and Bodhisattvas perform various levels of single-pointed concentration. Following the eight examples of the illusion of dream (rmi lam sgyu ma'i dpe rgyad brten nas) he purified the world, caused sentient beings to ripen and so on. Emptiness is not obscured by appearances nor are appearances stopped by emptiness. Even if the appearance of the collection of dependent originations is not stopped in the inseparable appearance and emptiness instantaneously, when it appears it is clearly visualized that nothing at all exists inherently. Thus he realized many doors of single-pointed concentration such as that of the single-pointed concentration of moving like a hero etc.

During the generation stage he immediately had a clear vision of the 32 deities and obtained realization of the teachings, thinking that he was not different from them. As soon as he meditated on the 'Possessor of the Wheel' (Guhyasamaja) and did the vajra recitation there arose the individual signs (of absorption) of the subtle energies of each of the five elements, such as the (vision like a) mirage and so on. He generated the absorptions of the dissolution of the three appearances: the signs of cherishing sentient beings—the signs of moon (-like white appearance), the sun (-like red increase) and the gloom (-like appearance of nearly attained). At the moment of the dissolution of the (gloom-like) nearly attained, he saw Bodhisattvas of the 10 stages making offerings to the Sambhogakaya Buddhas in Buddhafields in all 10 directions and all around him gods and goddesses made offerings to him while seated on cushions of sun and moon. He saw many heroes and heroines all around him who sang vajra songs and performed dances and so on, and inexpressible auspicious signs, but he was not impressed.

When meditating on the clear light ('od gsal) and illusory body (sgyu lus), he saw that the nature of the mind gone beyond is clear and empty as a cloudless sky and that the nature of the mind of great bliss and emptiness is the measure of light arising as the rainbow body. He saw the (body) mandala of the 32 deities inside his body and had visions of many inconceivable Buddhafields in great detail. Even though he did not meditate on the clear light of sleep, (his sleep was) held by it. He realized the meaning of the three characteristics and the three kisses of the Great Unification (zung 'jug).

At the time of the pure illusory body he went to Uddiyana (O rgyan) and saw a tent of five-colored rainbow light, in which Vajrayogini was surrounded by many heroes and heroines and at which he looked from the outside. When he moved above it, he saw many objects of enjoyment of many heroes and heroines.

At another time he intended to go to Tushita. He grasped a ray of moonlight and arrived there after a little while, but said that he did not actually see Tushita as he woke up too early from that sleep. He also went to the 'World of Joy' (Sukhavati) and said that he saw

1,000 Buddhas seated in a line there in a precious light palace. When he went to visit these Pure Buddhafields he either rode on a sun and moon (disc) or he grasped a light ray or rode on Garuda's back. Thus he could travel to the land of the dakinis by the power of his wish and then actually see them.

Once His Eminence Chökyi Gyaltsen Pal Zangpo said that if one wanted to ask a question but did not do so at that time, the master would later say that the matter is such-and-such. Later Buton Rinpoche answered his question on an occasion when he gave advice according to various teachings, and Jetsun Chökyi Gyaltsen felt great peace of mind. This is a definite sign of the clairvoyance of 'reading' other people's thoughts. Needless to say, there were many definite signs of the clairvoyance of (Buton Rinpoche).

The Master Acharya Arya then gave extensive explanations of the tantric commentaries and Buton studied the empowerments, teachings and oral instructions on Guhyasamaja in the traditions of Ngog Lotsawa and Marpa Lotsawa, as well as all the various implements and everything about Guhyasamaja in the tradition of Jnanapada (Yeshe Zhab). He also studied everything about Kalachakra in the tradition of Ra Lotsawa and Bromi Lotsawa, including the empowerments, teachings and oral instructions. He also studied Mayajala (sgyu dra) and the tantric commentary on Mayajala Vairocana. He also received the tantric commentary of Dra Nag (dgra nag) and so on about Yamantaka; the empowerments and so on in the Luipa tradition of Heruka; the empowerments and so on of Hevajra in the traditions of Sakya and of Ngog Lotsawa; the explanation of the empowerment of the Four Asanas (gdan bzhi) and the tantric explanations of the Space Yoga (rnal 'byor nam mka); the empowerment and Tantra of Mahamaya and so on about the Great Illusory One (sgyu ma chen po); the three Dohas and so on about the heart of the practice of the (maha)siddhas (grub pa grub snying); the empowerments of the 21 Taras; the teachings of the great Compassionate One (dmar khrid); the Yoga of the Vajra Sphere; the empowerment of the Immovable Buddha (mi 'khrugs pa) in the tradition of Atisha (Dipamkara Shri Jnana); the White Umbrella and so on of Usnishavijaya (gtsug tor); Amitayus in the tradition of Drub Gyalma (grub rgyal ma); Vidarana (rnam 'joms) in the tradition of Bari; the 'Four Shvana' and Hayagriva; the Three Objects etc. of Miyowa as well as various sadhanas, dharanis and sutras.

In short, from that master he received extensive good attainments based on the sutras and tantras. Especially in terms of Yoga Tantra he received the 'Tattvasamgraha' (de nyid bsdus pa), the 'Shekara' (rtse mo), the 'Shriparamadya' (dpal chog), the 'Vajradhatuvagishvara' (chos dbyings gsung bdan) and the 'Tantra of Purification' (sbyong rgyud) etc., including all their teachings of commentaries, empowerments and the oral instructions.

He became well versed in the practices of both the traditions of the upper (stod lugs) and lower (med lugs) methods and he became one of the greatest scholars of the three times. He considered this master to be truly Vajradhara and not even for one moment considered his master to be an ordinary person, even though this master actually addressed him as 'a Lord of Dharma'. He always praised his master and cited his opinions when giving teachings.

After requesting the Lamas Tishri Kunga Gyaltsen, Dönyö Gyaltsen, Sonam Gyaltsen and others for the mind of enlightenment, Buton Rinpoche cherished it. From the holy master Sonam Gyaltsen Pal Zangpo he received mainly the exposition of the empowerment of the Nairatmya (bdag med ma) and Trailokyavijaya (khams gsum rnam rgyal ma). Inbetween he studied Guru Yoga and so on. To be concise, from the time he studied astrology and grammar with the teacher Gyam Seng (rgyam seng), up to the time he studied the meaning of the Abhisamayalankara with the scholar Kunga Gyaltsen, he had already had 28 teachers, and he had great respect for all of them. In short, the great Buton who had so many qualities cherished the vessel of compassion and perfect wisdom and crossed the great ocean of the sutras and tantras, thus lifting up the jewel of the two purposes (of self and others) and made an end to the poverty of the mind of countless embodied beings beyond description, which is clear as soon as one investigates this.

This holy being perfected himself in the practice of Dharma and during the regular summer and winter terms continuously gave explanations of his own commentaries on the 'Abhismayalankara', the 'Abhidharmasamuccaya', the 'Discernment of the Aspects of Valid Cognition', and the 'Guide to the Bodhisattva's Way of Life' as well as the root texts and commentaries of monastic discipline (Vinaya), many expositions on the sutras and tantras as well as empowerments, transmissions and miscellaneous oral instructions and so on. During the spring and autumn courses he taught his own annotations on the Kalachakra Tantra and its Great Commentary. He also taught his own commentary on the 'Clear Lamp Commentary of Guhyasamaja', his 'Commentary on the Yoga-Vajrodaya' (yoga rdo rje 'byung ba), his commentary on the 'Glorious Samputa' (dpal sam bu ti), etc.

He also gave many teachings based on the sutras and tantras, empowerments, oral instructions, blessings and transmissions. In short, he was able to decide with certainty about a specific practice for each different person and to teach them the transmission, the reasonings and the oral instructions. Moreover, he composed many commentaries and explanations of commentaries and so on.

He wrote a 'History of Kalachakra, an 'Astrology Based on the Sphere of Phenomena' (chos 'byung rgyu mtshan sgrub), the 'Accomplishment of Grammar' (sgra sgrub), the 'Abbreviation of the First Commentary called Ears of Corn of the Definite Meaning' (mdor bsdus dang po'i tika nges don snye ma), the 'Sadhana of the Instant Arisal (lhan skyes kyi sgrub thabs), the 'Sadhana of the Heart Mandala' (thugs dkyil gyi sgrub thabs), the 'Sadhana of Full Completion' (yongs rdzogs kyi sgrub thabs), the 'Praise of Full Completion' (yongs rdzogs kyi bstod pa), the 'Ritual of the Last Period (dus tha ma'i cho ga), the 'Ritual of the (Self-initiation into the) Mandala' (dkyil chog), the 'Invocation Ritual' (rab gnas), the 'Burnt Offerings of the Four Activities' (las bzhi'i sbyin bsreg), the 'Pacifying Burnt Offerings' (zhi ba'i sbyin bsreg), the 'Explanation of the (Self-initiation into the) Mandala Ritual' (dkyil chog gi bshad pa), a 'Commentary on the Abbreviated Empowerment' (dbang mdor bstan gyi tika), the 'Preparatory Practices of the Instructions (khrid kyi snog 'gro), the 'Virtue of the Beginning' (thog dge), the 'Virtue of the Middle' (bar dge), the 'Virtue of the End' (mthar dge), an 'Introduction' (ngo sprod), the 'Abbreviated Meaning' (dsdus don), the 'Refutation of Contraversions' ('gal spong), the 'Basic Lines' (thig rtsa), the 'Astrology of Practice' (lag len rtsis) and a 'Garland of Offerings' (mchod phreng).

About Guhyasamaja he composed the 'Clear Lamp Commentary' (sgron gsal gyi tika), the 'Abbreviated Meaning of the Sphere of Phenomena' (chos 'byung bsdus don), the 'Teaching' (khrid yig), the 'Sadhana' (sgrub thabs), the 'Mandala Ritual' (dkyil chog), the 'Requests to the Lineage Gurus of the Teachings' (dmar khrid brgyud pa'i gsol 'debs), the 'Requests to the Lineage Gurus of the Tantric Commentary' (rgud 'grel brgyud pa'i gsol 'debs), the 'Praise of the Mandala' (dkyil 'khor gyi bstod pa), the 'Offering of the Ritual Cakes' (gtor chog), the 'Sadhana of Guhyasamaja of Manjushri Vajra' ('jam rdor gyi sgrub thabs) and the mandala rituals.

After the emanation of the Lord Manjughosha Dragpa Gyaltsen

and his brother, Lama Donyö Gyaltsen, requested Buton Rinpoche for teachings on Hevajra, he composed the commentary on the transmission of 'The Practice of Hevajra'. While writing this commentary the great Dragpa Gyaltsen met the venerable Buton Rinpoche twice. The first time they met when he was coming from outside into the lower floor. The second time was in the evening of the full moon of the spring month (Feb.-Mar.) of the year of the male water monkey (1332). Jetsun Dragpa Gyaltsen appeared wearing a white robe tied with a girdle of fine dark red cloth round his waist and a woolen shawl. His hair was combed in a fringe on his forehead and, descending from the top floor, he met him in the middle storey. They had a long conversation about the Dharma and the great Jetsun Dragpa Gyaltsen mentioned that he would be very pleased if the commentary was written and the sutras and commentaries of the general teachings of Lord Buddha and especially of the teachings on secret mantra would be revised (zhus dag mdsad pa). Dragpa Gyaltsen said: "Even though I particularly intended to correct my own teachings, I have not been able to do so yet, but please would you do this?"

Buton Rinpoche reflected on the fact that he had had a vision of meeting with this great master Jetsun Dragpa Gyaltsen and that there was no one closer to the lineage of the Sakyapas and the practice of Hevajra then himself. This was a prophetic indication to write a commentary. He remained detached even though he had been requested to check the many commentaries of the Hierarch and refute or establish them. He then composed his commentary (lung 'grel).

Lama Sonam Gyaltsen Pal Zangpo requested him to compose a commentary about the Samputa and he considered this, but for some time the Dakinis did not give him permission to do so. He then offered ritual cakes and offerings and made requests and, after receiving the signs of them granting him permission, he composed the 'Commentary on the Samputa'. He also composed an 'Abbreviation of the Commentary on the Samputa' (bsdus don) and a 'Small Text on the Emanation Mandala' ('phrul 'khor gyi dpe chung), a 'Great Commentary on Clear Realization' (mngon rtogs chen po), the 'Sadhana of Samvara' (sdom 'byung gi sgrub thabs) and various 'Mandala Rituals' (dkyil chog) and so on. Furthermore, he composed 'Friendly Letters to Various Persons such as the King of Dharma Sonam De' and 'Answers to the Questions' of Yagde Panchen and Lama Rinchen Yeshe, as well as a large collection of instructive letters to students. He wrote 'Stages of Dharma Practice for Beginners' (las dang po pa'i chos spyod kyi rim pa).

The great lord Dragpa Gyaltsen and his sons, Lord Kunga Dondrub and Lord Yeshe Kunga, and his grandsons, Lord Konchog Gyaltsen and Lord Ngodrub Gyaltsen Pal Zangpo, cherished the good customs of their paternal ancestors. They especially honored the precious Lord of Dharma Buton Rinpoche by maintaining the temple founded by their forefather, and looked after the great Sangha community. In particular, when Lord Kunga Dondrub constructed the inconceivable mansions of the mandalas of Yoga Tantra, the great Lord of Dharma himself drew the plan for the following mandalas: 213 mandalas of the root tantras, 129 mandalas of the explanatory tantras, 84 mandalas of the glorious supreme tantras (dpal mchog), 12 mandalas of the training tantras and, furthermore, 37 mandalas of the 'Ornament of Vajra Essence' (rdo rje snying po rgyan), 24 and 19 mandalas of the 'Empowerment of the Speech of the Sphere of Existence (chos dbyings gsung gi dbang bhug) and the 100,000 Meditation Buddhas of Ushnishavijaya.

He also printed the great collection of the translations of the commentaries, including the entire text, and completing the ones that were previously incomplete. He condensed the ones that were too long and compiled a catalogue which classified them.

He composed a 'General History of the Yoga Tantra' (yoga spyi'i chos 'bhung), a 'Commentary on the History of the Vajra' (rdo rje 'byung ba tika), a 'Vajrasattva Sadhana' (rdo rje sems dpa'i sgrub thabs), the 'Practice of the Vajra' (rdo rje 'byung ba'i lag len), the 'Basic Lines' (thig rtsa), a 'Garland of Offerings (mchod bhreng), 'Burnt Offerings' (sbyin bsreg), the 'Mandala Ritual of Kun Rig' (kun rig gi dkyil chog), the 'Burnt Offering of a Garland of Offerings' (mchod phreng sbyin bsreg), the 'Burning of Corpses' (ro bsreg), the 'Mandala Ritual of Ushnishavijaya', (gtsug dgu'i dkyil chog) and the 'Mandala Ritual of the Empowerment of the Speech of the Sphere of Existence' (chos dbyings gsung dbang gi dkyil chog), the 'Mandala Ritual of Tsemo (rtse mo'i dkyil chog), the 'Mandala Ritual of the Glorious Supreme One' (dpal mchog gi dkyil chog) and others besides.

He also furnished the instructions for a great temple with an inner image of the great lord with the proportions of the Jowo statue and completely filled it with the relics of the Tathagatas, including images of the 16 Great Arhats. On the walls he painted the 'Lives of Lord Buddha as a Bodhisattva' (byang chub sems pa'i skyes rabs), the 'Twelve Great Deeds of Lord Buddha' (mdzad pa bcu gnyis), the 'Exposition of the Miracles Performed by Lord Buddha' (cho 'phrul chen po ston pa), the 'Clear Expression of the Realizations of the Good Magada' (magata bzang mo'i rtogs brjod) and the 'Meeting of the Father and Son' (yab sras mjal ba), the Painting of Udrayana and other images. Furthermore, he had statues created of the Meditation Buddhas of the various classes of Tantra.

Inside the temple that was erected by the Lord of Dharma himself, he built a statue of Kalachakra of various precious substances. This was filled inside with the essence of relic pills of the Tathagatas and decorated with various precious ornaments. It blazed with the major and minor marks of a Buddha's body and was aglow with light rays radiating from it. He also made the designs for cast images of Vairocana, Guhyasamaja and the great Shakyamuni Buddha and so on, sculptures of the Vajradhatu (rdor dbyings) and paintings of the 84 Mahasiddhas.

When he was invited to Zhangs by the great leader Gyaltsen Zangpo, he erected stupas symbolic of the Dharmakaya, such as the 'Stainless Stupa', and images of the Nirmanakayas of the great Shakyamuni Buddha and images of the Sambhogakayas of Maitreya and Manjushri etc. He also designed many mandalas of Carya Tantra such as the four mandalas for the conferral of the empowerment of Vajrapani, the three mandalas of the White, Blue and Green Vairocana, Yamantaka, the five mandalas of the Wrathful Conqueror of the Three Realms, the five mandalas of the Victor Miyowa, three mandalas of the Root Tantra of Manjushri, three mandalas of the Three Samaya Commitments, the mandala of the Five Protectors, the four mandalas of the One Endowed with Light Rays, the four mandalas of the White Umbrella, the mandala of the Treatises on the Planets (gza' yum), the mandala of the Collector and so on, and he compiled their collected works.

He designed the nine subtle mandalas of the rituals of Avalokiteshvara, the subtle mandala of the ritual of the One With A Thousand Eyes, the mandala for the various activities relating to Arya Tara, two mandalas of Vajrapani Beneath the Earth, the five mandalas of Supreme Knowledge (rig pa mchog), the mandala of the Subduer of Spirits ('byung po), the four mandalas of the Supreme Dancer, the mandala of the Lotus-like One, the mandala of the Lotus-crowned One and so on, and compiled the collected works of the Kriyatantra.

Moreover, he composed a 'Sadhana of the Five Deities of Red

Yamantaka' (gshed dmar lha lnga'i sgrub thabs) and the mandala rituals and blessing rituals. He wrote an extensive and a short 'Sadhana of the Great Illusive One' (maha maya) and the mandala rituals. He also compiled an extensive, medium and short 'General Presentation of the Classes of Tantra' (rgyud sde'i spyi'i rnam gzhag). He composed many commentaries, such as the 'Annotations to the Ritual Activities of Monastic Discipline' ('dul ba'i las chog gi mchan bu), after which he wrote the 'Great Life-tree of the Precious Doctrine' (bstan pa rin po che'i srog shing chen po).

In the temple he built he collected most of the works containing the words of Lord Buddha (ka gyur), such as the 'Collected Works on Tantra' (rgyud 'bum) and the 'Transmissions of Monastic Discipline' ('dul ba lung). He collected the large, middle and small 'Perfection of Wisdom Sutra' written in gold and most of the great (Indian) commentaries, as well as most of the commentaries that were written by the excellent Tibetan spiritual teachers.

During the day he gave Dharma teachings and at night he conferred empowerments until his eyes turned red. Even though they would turn white again in the morning, he would merely say: "Ha ha, today I have become old." Without any grief or fatigue he would perform the work of the Dharma and, as he cherished each individual disciple, he had no free time at all.

Amongst his students there were people of all nationalities as they came from India, China, Nepal, Turkestan, North of Amdo, Mongolia, Ga, Central Tibet, Tsang, Kham (mdo stod) and Amdo (mdo smad) and so on, and he ripened and liberated many of them. He gathered many students such as the emanation of the Protector Manjughosha, who held the stainless lineage of the Sakyapa lords of Dharma, Jampa'i Yang Donyö Gyaltsen Pal Zangpo ('jam pa'i dbyangs don yod rgyal mtshan), the teacher of all transmigrating beings Sonam Gyaltsen Pal Zangpo (bsod nams rgyal mtshan) and the great teacher Sonam Lodrö Gyaltsen Pal Zangpo (bsod nams blo gros rgyal mtshan) and his brother, as well as the Bodhisattva Sonam Drag and the learned Master Chö Trag Pal Zangpo Gushri (chos grags dpal bzang po gu shri), the translator Lo Drö Pal (blo gros dpal) and other learned, noble and excellent ones. To some of his countless students he would teach only philosophy for a while and to others he explained only the lineages of Tantra. He had countless students who studied Abhisamayalankara, Bodhisattvacaryavatara and Vinaya and also the text and commentaries of Madhyamika, Pramana and Abhidharma, together with the Panchavim-shatisahasrikaloka (rgyab chos), and they became very learned in the meaning of these teachings.

Other students studied Guhyasamaja according to Arya (Nagarjuna), Yoga and Kalachakra ('phag, yog, dus) and in the tantras of Mahakala, Hevajra and Samputa (gur, rtags, sam) as well as in the systems of Luipa, Krishna and Ghantapada (lo, nag, dril) and the three traditions of Krishnayamari-Bhairava (nag 'jigs skor gsum) etc. and they became very learned in the meaning of these teachings. Still other students became great yogis who accomplished stability in the generation and completion stages (bskyed rdzogs rim) and the practice of Kusuli and so forth. In the great monastic institutions he acted as the principal of as many as 3,800 Sangha-members. In Riphug only holders of the great scriptures of philosophy and tantra and meditating monks gathered together, about 500 Sangha-members who stayed in strict retreat.

Furthermore, at Tagtshal Ormo (stag tshal 'or mo), at Nyemo Tshalmig (snye mo'i tshal mig), at Tredre Yul (gre 'bras yul), at Shang Je Mar (shangs dbye dmar) and so on, he instructed many tens of thousands of people in the mind of enlightenment while planting the seed of liberation and causing them to bring their cyclic existence to an end.

At this time the glorious holy master, the protector of transmigrating beings Sonam Gyaltsen Pal Zangpo invited the great Lord of Dharma (Buton) to the great monastery of the glorious Sakya and listened to his instructions in the three stages of the vehicles in terms of Sutra and Tantra.

Furthermore, he extensively benefited the scholars and caused them to hold many great scriptures completely in mind. In brief, people everywhere heard of this great Bodhisattva who was unique and whose fame pervaded throughout the Asian continent.

The universal emperor of China, Thogon Thimur Gan, and the Dharma King Punyamala of India and others inquired about the physical health of this great life-tree of the doctrine, the great master Buton Rinpoche, the regent of Shakyamuni. They also made inquiries about his mental discomforts and contentments, his journeys and his holy activities in the letters which they sent and which were always accompanied by presents. He answered them in letters with gifts of the profound Dharma and these were read in all directions. Everywhere these letters were regarded highly.

As an imperial convoy was about to invite him to go to China, the Lord of Dharma foresaw this. With his clairvoyance he directly perceived that on the first day of the first month of the monkey year (1344) a discussion took place before the emperor, that on the first day of the third month an edict was written and that on the 15th day of the ninth month envoys led by important Mongols from Turkestan called Bhade Tshengben and Dzambala Tushri Gon (bha de tsheng dben dzambhala tu shri mgon) would arrive. He only mentioned that he saw an envoy of invitation come in dreams and he checked to see whether going this would be beneficial for sentient beings or not. Upon seeing that the time to subdue these beings had not yet come, he remained in retreat, mainly performing meditations on his Meditation Buddha until the messengers of the envoy returned in the tenth month.

In the meantime he translated the rest of the commentary of Durgasingha (drakalapa) called 'Kalapavyakarana' (durga seng ba'i 'phro) and he wrote an extensive commentary on this. Apart from this, he made fundamental translations such as the '360 Commentaries which Present Abbreviations of Empowerments' (dbang mdor bstan gyi dka' 'grel sum brgya drug bcu pa), the 'Commentary on the Vajra Nectar' (rdo rje bdud rtsi'i dka' 'grel) by Acharya Amogagarbha (dri med snying po), the 'Commentary which Adorns the Vajra Essence' rdo rje snying po rgyan gyi dka' 'grel) by Vimalamitra (rab zhi bshes gnyen), the 'Commentary on the Sadhana of Vajrasattva' by Lalitavajra, the 'Commentary on Abbreviations' (mdor byas kyi 'grel pa) by Vibhuti, the 'Clear Lamp Commentary' (sgron gsal gyi dka' 'grel) by Thug Je Zhab (thugs rje zhabs), the 'Commentary on the Five Stages' (rim lnga'i 'grel pa) by Muni Shri and the 'Commentary on Difficult Progress' (bgrod dka'i 'grel pa) by Chan Sum Bang (spyan gsum 'bangs) and so on. Thus he translated many commentaries. He also translated the 'Ritual of Avalokiteshvara called Don Zhags' which had been partially translated earlier and corrected deficiencies in the 'Commentary on the Five Stages' written by Abhaya and translated by Vibhuti. He also made the translation of the 'Great Tantra of the Glorious Non-dualistic Ushnishavijaya' (dpal gnyis su med pa rnam par rgyal ba'i rgyud chen po) in which he was encouraged and sponsored by the great Lama Kunpang (kun spangs), and he refuted all the false tantric treatises.

Thus on the one hand he translated the great sutras and their commentaries and on the other hand he revised earlier translations with the original Sanskrit texts and corrected their defects, thus enacting the deeds of a great life-tree of the doctrine. In short, although he made translations from the whole range of writers and at the same time wrote different kinds of commentaries, not one of the scribes who surrounded him was without work and he dictated to them without hesitation. He mastered the texts in terms of ultimate and relative reality (ji lta ji snyed pa'i don la dbang 'byor). Whenever he used his voice he experienced the blooming of the channels wheel at the throat and he could immediately remember the commentaries and the letters with Dharma instructions. He could remember many things that others did not and, memorizing something only once, he would never forget it thereafter.

Travelling here and there, he gave empowerments, explanations and instructions which came directly to his mind without having to consult a book. Because of all the above, he became a fully qualified Buddha and was far more special then all the Bodhisattvas and Tantrikas (of his time). The great Buton did not experience pride even once and never acted contrary to humility. No matter how close one stayed to him, one would never even once think of any of his behavior as being irregular. He had an extremely deep mental disposition for the deeds of a devout person. All year round he would not take a rest from giving many empowerments, explanations, teachings and oral transmissions to others. On top of his meditations on the Meditation Buddhas with and without signs, he constantly made offerings of clay statues (tsa tsa) of water and of ritual cakes and so on without fatigue.

When he was 58 years old he fell slightly ill and everyone offered him medicines and their service as attendants, whereupon Buton Rinpoche said: "One who does not know how to use adverse conditions in the path to enlightenment is not a practitioner. A time will come when nothing at all helps anymore. Why should one not die at any time? You should not be alarmed. Even if all of you would serve as my attendants, I would still die. And if not, if one has lived virtuously, what could be the problem?" He entered meditation and, after increasing his single-pointed concentration further, his physical elements regained their strength.

Although he had inconceivable signs of accomplishments, both perceived and seen in dreams, he never spoke of them in public and did not stop increasing his collections (of merit and wisdom). Some great meditators speak of the signs of accomplishment to others, but clairvoyance or the ability to perform miracles are signs of the devil (maras) if they are not based on a realization of the mind. And if one understands the mind, there is no need for these signs. As he possessed unobstructed clairvoyance which saw the meaning of all hidden phenomena directly, he wisely pretended that he needed to exert himself to know things that were nearby. He would ask questions to those around him like, "What is that?"

Although he never said that one should keep one's distance from people indulging in talk such as, "My teacher is good and yours is not," or, "This practice of mine is profound and that practice is not profound," he integrated his advice in his manner of teaching where he generally taught: "The practice is spoiled by giving in to such criticism. It is one thing to spoil the food with goats' fat, but by criticizing a spiritual master or a practice, others may regard one's criticism as correct! In general one does not elevate oneself by slandering others and it also increases attachment and hatred, but one should be particularly afraid of the slander derived from being prejudiced towards practices or practitioners, as there is no greater difficulty than that which is called hell.

"In general, there is no meaning in filling up one's free time this way and it has many disadvantages. Especially when one compares the essence of the transmissions, it shows lack of respect. Such actions are based on attachment, hatred and jealousy and cause great downfall. Particularly for practitioners like us, who still are worldly practitioners and say that we do not do these things, abuse and loss of faith come easily."

When the sponsor Alcam asked how he could find certainty about the practice, Buton Rinpoche answered: "As a result of the realization that a precious human rebirth is difficult to obtain, great enthusiastic perseverance will be generated. If one knows that one may die soon, one gives up attachment and aversion relating to this life. If one knows the relation between one's actions and their results, one abandons even the smallest unwholesome activity. If one knows about the suffering of cyclic existence one immediately generates the wish to be liberated. If one knows that all sentient beings are one's father and mother, one generates great compassion. If one knows that all things are empty, one generates the wisdom that understands the actual mode of existence. One avoids all harmful activities even at the cost of one's life and if one ever does lose control, one confesses it with regret and causes others to act similarly.

"If one is endowed with these qualities, one will become an Arya being who has abandoned harming anyone and engages in pure behavior. Without neglecting even one small wholesome activity, one generates faith in the Three Jewels. One meditates to understand the relation between activities and their results, good and bad. If one has these three qualities, one is a practitioner. If one practices as many wholesome activities as possible and wishes to reach Buddhahood for the welfare of others, and if one meditates on the emptiness of object, subject and action and dedicates everything to enlightenment for the sake of all sentient beings, one is a true Bodhisattva, irrespective of one's appearance.

"If one has the highest self-discipline and thereby has become a fully qualified Lord, and if one meditates on one's body as the body of a Meditation Buddha, on one's speech as mantra and on one's mind as the great seal (Mahamudra), one is a tantrika by virtue of these four qualities."

Some people criticized Buton Rinpoche's teaching, saying that it was diffuse, superficial, and without essence like a garland. "He says many things which he should not say, he listens to many things he should not listen to and he collects many things he should not collect," they said.

Hearing this Buton Rinpoche was dissatisfied. He spoke of this reaction, saying: "The water of good qualities attaches to the tree trunk of pride. I do not know where this profound instruction came from, but it is not something about which the Bodhisattvas have failed to give advice. If even the great Aryas who abide in the stages are not satisfied with their studies, why should we not engage in extensive studies? If we collect mental imprints in our mind by limitless studies, this will become a cause for teaching the Dharma to limitless sentient beings in accordance with their level of mind.

"When, for instance, we perform service to the Gongma, we create a great mandala in colored sand of, for example, the Shriparamadyakulasamgraha and of the Vajradhatuvagoshvara, after which merely hearing the name of a certain mandala of Kriya, Charya, or Yoga Tantra or merely seeing it is beneficial for purifying a lot of karma and obscurations. We should try to accomplish these even though it may be difficult," he said.

He treated the Geshes and officials and humble beggars who desired the Dharma equally, imparting to them all an equal share of the Dharma, with an even mind, without self-interest and with the same feelings for all. He was never attached to common possessions, food or clothing and whenever he received wealth he used it as offerings to Lord Buddha or ordered it to be given to sentient beings. Although he would eat any food, tasty or not, he did not regard it as food but something to make it easier for others to serve and to practice the doctrine.

Many Meditation Buddhas showed their faces to him and he saw them as clearly as a constellation of stars, in which there was not even one that he did not know. Yet there was never any vanity or haughtiness in his mind. Whatever empowerment he conferred, he did not need to perform any special service. When he brought the Wisdom Beings of the empowerment down, great waves of inspiration were experienced, and he generated various single-pointed concentrations. One day when he conferred the empowerment of Heruka in the wintertime on the occasion of the new year, two long ears of corn sprang from his ritual vase; the ritual substances started to boil and the lamps burnt brightly without becoming dim and many other wonderful signs appeared. Blessed water poured forth miraculously on dry land and there were reports of the great Dharma Protectors who guard the doctrine talking to him as he would do to people.

Altogether this biography of the great Buton Rinpoche is inconceivable and inexpressible. If one saw his books on philosophy and mantra, one would have thought that he spent his whole life studying them; if one thought of his students, the ordained ones, the novices (dge tshul) and fully ordained monks (dge slong) and so on, it seemed as if he had spent his whole life in teaching and conferring precepts and vows as an abbot and teacher.

If one thought of the disciples who became great teachers, it seemed as if he had spent his whole life giving teachings. If one saw the students who possessed full insight, it seemed as if he had spent his entire life guiding scholars. If one thought of his clairvoyance in reading other beings' minds and the full inquiries of single-pointed concentration, it seemed as if he had spent his whole life meditating. If one thought of his visions of the face of the Meditation Buddhas and the capacity and power involved, it seemed as if he had spent his whole life meditating on the generation stage and mantra recitation.

If one looked at the sermons he prepared, it seemed as if he had spent his entire life writing. If one looked at the statues that he erected, it seemed as if he spent his entire life making statues. If one looked at his translations of the holy Dharma, it seemed as if he had spent his whole life translating, and if one looked at the great commentaries that he composed, it seemed as if he had spent his whole life writing commentaries. If one looked at his conferral of empowerments, it seemed as if he spent his whole life conferring empowerments. If one looked at the stupas that he built, it seemed as if he spent his entire life making stupas and the same with the clay statues (tsha tsha), water offerings (chab gtor) and so on, so that one may wonder whether he would have had the time to do anything else.

In short, this holy person fully trained himself in very many scriptures and transmissions of Sutra and Tantra and became truly admirable. He translated texts that had not been translated before and revised earlier translations. He repaired deficiencies and elucidated the meaning in commentaries. He gave transmissions of all the common and uncommon profound practices, as a mother grants her only son the hidden wealth of his father. He looked after a huge assembly of disciplined practitioners in the world.

He had a great love, even in his sleep, for all his students, the simple ones as well as those with a clear mind; for those who were diligent and understood things with a minimum of information as well as those who needed to be led through every word; for those who stayed at a distance as well as those who stayed close to him; for those who were old and had acquired qualities as well as those who first started as new students; for those who made many offerings and those who needed to scramble for a living. He treated them all with love and compassion, with joy and equanimity, and looked after them with the great loving kindness of a mother for her only child.

Casting out attachment to the pleasures of food, clothing, housing, bedding and wealth, he used these for the temporary and ultimate benefit of others and served them even at the risk of his own life. To see where and in which way he could plant the seed of full liberation, he listened to others and with clear ability and pure, suitable words he would teach them without any adulteration. He taught happiness for more than 40 years, ripening beings and placing them on the path to liberation. The instructions transmitted from mouth to mouth, ear to ear and heart to heart are powerful methods that have the capacity to turn even negative people into Buddhas within one perfect human lifetime, or to cause them to attain Buddhahood within seven or 16 subsequent lives.

Thus, with these vast and profound instructions that were taught by Lord Buddha and gathered by the collectors, explained by the Bodhisattvas and handed down through a succession of accomplished ones in an unbroken lineage, which carry a continuous mist of blessings and the swirling breath of the Dakinis, very many fortunate people were ripened and liberated by him.

In a pure biography like this one, there is no exaggeration nor falsehood, nor any deprecation of truths. Only things that are true are recorded here and things that did not happen are not mentioned. This holy person, who went beyond the objects of enjoyment of ordinary persons' minds, only worked for the purpose of others and held the doctrine and sentient beings as his only objects. In the process he also obtained everything he needed and abandoned every object of abandonment without exception. Having performed extensive deeds for the precious doctrine of Lord Buddha, and holding the great victory banner so that the doctrine would not decline, he wished to make it spread even more. This can be clearly seen now by everybody.

In the year of the iron female hare (1351), when the Lord of Dharma was 62 years old, in order to reconcile the fights between the Ya and the Phag (gya' phag), he went to the kingdom of Nyima U (nyi ma dbus) and on his way he gave many Hinayana and Mahayana teachings in Nyangtö Chumig (myang stod chu mig), Ralung and so on. He acted as Abbot and Acharya to many fully ordained monks, novices and lay vow holders, including the Abbot of Tsi, Namkha Rinchen Pal Zangpo (nam mkha' rin chen dpal bzang po).

He cured the mute son of Rasog Lhatsun by changing his name. Through the blessings and dependent causation involved, the son was able to speak. In the country of Nyangtö he imparted the instructions for the generation of the mind of enlightenment to many people and planted the seeds for liberation and omniscience. Following the pathways along the narrow ridges at Gyadrag kaba, Khamova, Langro gadpa, Semig byispa, Gurpochethri, Kyikhu Jagpa (rgya brag ka ba, kha mo va, glang ro gad pa, se mig byis pa, 'gur po che khri, skyid khud jag pa) etc. on the way to Kharo, he introduced many people to the Dharma.

Proceeding on this journey he arrived at Kharo, where he benefitted very many beings, connecting them with the holy Dharma. From there he went to Yabrog (ya 'brog). At Nakartse (sna dkar rtse) in Yabrog he acted as Abbot and teacher for many fully ordained monks, novices and lay vow holders. He imparted the mind of enlightenment to many people and caused them to put an end to their cyclic existence. In Yabrog he crossed the great lake Tsomo Che in a boat, and inside the boat he compared the time of the tradition of the rules of monastic discipline (Vinaya) with the Abhidharmakosha.

Then he went to Do where he again gave many teachings on the profound and vast practices. After that he went to the Rabtsun Temple in Gan Jangthang (gan byang thang) and to Mount Drangsong Rinpoche Ri, the Temple of Drathang (gra thang), the temples in Yanglung (yang klung rnam rgyal) and to the blue Nedong Palace (pho brang do sngo), to the Temple of Thrabrug (phra 'brug), to the Bugudo Palace (phrobrang yu gu do), to the Temple of Olkha Tsathang ('ol kha tsha thang) and so on, where he helped many people such as Lobpon Jangchub Gyaltsen Tai Situ and others to put an end to their cyclic existence, by teaching them the vast and profound Hinayana and Mahayana practices of philosophy and Tantra. He gave empowerments, explanations and instructions as well as many explanations and transmissions of philosophy. Acting as Abbot and teacher to many fully ordained monks, novices and male and female lay vow holders, he extensively performed each and every single action of the precious doctrine, without ever raising his voice.

He then went to the land of Tongde (stong sde) in Dagpo, where he stayed with Lama Sonam Gyaltsen Pal Zangpo. On his way there he had to spend two days travelling in the snow mountains at La Chenpo. Although all the old and young people dug holes in the, snow they still slipped and fell down while walking, and on top of that Sonam Senge and the other benefactors developed a strong doubt whether the Lord of Dharma would be able to proceed. Their faith was severely shaken, but they were surrounded by the great Dharma Protectors and even the Nine-headed Demon of the 'place of the revolting enemies' and the 'Boastful One' and so on accompanied and served the Lord of Dharma. They escorted him and rendered him service. Even though they stayed in desolate places, no hindrances occurred whatsoever, and Buton Rinpoche was helped by an enormous gathering of people who came from nobody knew where. Also, the robber chief Chogpa Ngothur (chogs pa sngo thur) and others accompanied him and escorted and served him well.

At that time, in the middle of a huge crowd of people in a market place in the land of Chade in Dagpo, was a giant woman from Tsang, whose body was twice the size of normal people. She wore a silk coat with the color of a parrot and multicolored ornaments in the fashion of the ladies from Tsang. She came with her servants from somewhere unknown and said: "Oh villagers, tomorrow in the early morning a very noble and perfect spiritual teacher will come to the country of Mangrong. If you build a bridge, welcome him and escort him on his way, your collections will be completed, impurities will be removed and a great store of merit will be achieved." She then disappeared and to an unknown place.

Although everyone was surprised, all the people went to the land of Mangrong that early morning, constructed wooden bridges over the steep slopes and cleared the path. They invited him to come across the bridges they had built and carried him across streams and took him in boats over the larger rivers. They requested his blessing and served him well.

All the followers then agreed that the woman must have been the Lady of Riphug, and the Lord of Dharma said, "Whosoever she may be, Arya Tara has afforded protection from the danger of water." When he set out in a boat, it was as if the waves of the river Tsangpo were tilted into the sky. The evil gods and nagas became angry and caused a storm that obscured the sky, so that they could not proceed. Then the Lord of Dharma performed an offering of ritual cakes and recited the words of the truth. The storm then completely subsided and all the teachers and students were able to proceed comfortably and increased their faith.

Next he was welcomed in the Fortress of the Good Naga (mkhar klu bzang) in Dagpo Dzom. When the faithful people set out to invite the master, the people from Rong stopped them with their soldiers and they could not give the invitation. Then in the centre of the land of that army, a fierce and frightening flash of lightning descended, by which a huge walnut tree was cracked into hundreds and thousands of pieces. The word spread that this happened because of the anger of the Sakyapas and everyone was afraid. Thus they had the power to overcome the people from Rong and they all developed faith in Buton Rinpoche. He was then able to instruct many people from Dagpo in the Mahayana teachings, such as Brum and Gomtsig and so on, and he planted the victory banner that did not allow the precious doctrine to decline in the land of Dagpo. In the east of Dagpo he acted as the Abbot and teacher to many holy people such as Gampoi Rinpoche Chökyi Senge, and he put limitless transmigrating beings on the path of liberation, by giving them many teachings on the stages of the (three) vehicles, empowerments and instructions.

He also wrote the 'Jewel Rosary of Precious Explanations of

Dedications' (bsngo ba'i gran bshad norbu rinpoche 'i phreng ba) and other works. Having been invited again, the master went back to central Tibet where, at the great monastery of Phagdru Thel (phag gru thel), he connected gatherings of hundreds and thousands of people, such as the spiritual teacher Lhatsun Sonam Oser and many Geshes, officials, meditating monks and male and female listeners and others, with the various practices of the Hinayana and Mahayana, leading them all through the dependent originations and placing them on the stages of liberation and omniscience.

He wrote down the 'Instructions of Dedications with Three Pure Aspects' (dam pa gsum ldan gyi bsno ba'i yi ge). Further, the Lord of Dharma was invited by the studying and meditating monks of all the small and big temples and hermitages at Yerpa, Gungthang, Phrulnang, Ramoche, Tshurphu, Janguri, Zhukum Garaba, Nyemo Thaling, Gyaba Dophug (yer pa,[20] gung thang, 'phrul snang, ra mo che, mtshur phu, byang u ri, gzhu kun dga' ra ba, snye mo tshal mig, gya ba mdo phug) and so on, where he gave teachings on philosophy and mantra which he had not given before and elaborated on teachings he had given before. In this way he ripened and liberated many fortunate people by means of their connection with the holy Dharma.

Many Geshes from the borderlands thought that they themselves were very learned and spoke divisive words. Some asked questions about Tantra and some about philosophy, but when Buton Rinpoche answered all their questions correctly he put an end to all their doubts and on top of that increased their faith.

Then he went again to Riphug where he wrote a 'Rosary of Offerings to Kunrig' (kun rig gi mchod phreng) and a 'Pacifying Burnt Offering to Kunrig' (kun rig zhi ba'i sbyin sreg). He also translated the 'Commentary on the Kalapa Exposition of Terms' (sgra'i bstan bcos kalapa'i 'grel pa) and the Tshadawa by Tilopa. He wrote a 'Root Commentary on the Sutra on Monastic Discipline' ('dul ba mdo rtsa'i ti ka) and started the 'One Hundred Thousand Stories' (gleng 'bum).

When the great leader Namkha Tanpa'i Gyaltsen Pal Zangpo was ordained, he gave him the name Rinchen Pal Zangpo, and in a similar fashion he acted as the Abbot and teacher to many fully ordained monks, novices and lay vow holders and so forth. He taught all of them continually on the Abisamayalankara, the Ascertainment, the Abidharmasamuccaya, the Root Sutra, the Bodhisattvacaryavatara, Kalachakra, Guhyasamaja, Vajrayogini and so forth. He also continually nurtured them with teachings on the 'Six Preparatory Practices' (sbyor drug), the 'Five Stages' (sa sde lnga), the 'Six Yogas of Naropa' (chos drug), the 'Self Healing' (ngal gso), 'Pacifying Practices' (zhi byed) and so forth.

He conferred empowerments in the Kriya, Charya, Yoga and Anuttarayoga tantras, in the Father, Mother and No-dual tantras, and gave the teachings and blessings of these without interruption. Thus he accomplished the welfare of limitless transmigrating beings in an extensive manner.

In the year of the male water monkey (1352), when he was 63 years old, he translated the treatise on the proportions of the glorious monastic university of Drepung and wrote a treatise on the proportions of the Mahabodhi according to the method of the Vimala commentary (byang chub chen po'i chag tshad dri med 'grel pa'i lugs). He thought about the way to benefit both the doctrine and many sentient beings and especially reflected on an outer monument for his mother. He decided that he would erect an excellent support of a Tathagata's Dharmakaya (stupa).

All the monks, both the new and old students and the donor, requested him to erect the stupa somewhere in the Zhalu market place. Buton Rinpoche answered them, saying: "There is always a risk that you may be plagued with illness or death and, if that were to happen, people will say that it is due to the stupa. Because of such words the stupa will become a circumstance for their accumulation of negativity. Therefore we will erect it in Riphug." It so happened that Lord Konchog Gyaltsen (dkon mchog rgyal mtshan) died and everyone understood that he possessed clairvoyance.

He then undertook an elaborate earth ritual of the Vajra shekara (rdo rdje stse mo'i sa chog rgyas pa). Based on astrological predictions about the conjunctions of the moon and the star Bya ze, he performed the full preparation of the site on the 23rd day of the third Tibetan month, which is the middle month of spring, and the foundation for the stupa was laid then.

Based on astrological predictions about the conjunctions of the sun and the star Sog pa, the stupa was to be built in bricks on the 3rd day of the 11th month, the first month of winter. It was 69 cubits of his own forearm in height and 23 cubits in width. Inside they placed 3,000 statues of Buddha Mitrugpa and more than 1,000 of Buddha Shakyamuni. Furthermore, it contained 300,000 clay statues with the dharani of Ushnishavijaya (gtsug tro dri med), more than 500,000 clay statues without dharani, and many clay statues with the relics of Tathagatas that still increased in number.

Clay statues were added containing the hair, bones, relics and pieces of the clothes of the pandit scholars and siddhas from India, Kashmir and Nepal. Also, clay statues containing the hair and bone relics of many Tibetan scholars and siddhas, as well as all kinds of objects carrying blessings from India, China, Kashmir, Nepal and Tibet as well as the mandalas of Ozer Drimed ('od zer dri med) and Ushnishavijaya (gtsug tor dri med) and so forth made from the earth of many holy places, were put inside the vase of the stupa, together with holy objects.

In short, the stupa was completely filled with piled-up relics of the Tathagatas and was encircled on the outside by 1,000 statues of Buddha Shakyamuni and 1,000 statues of Buddha Mitrugpa. Besides this, different stupas were built such as the 'Granting Long Life Stupa' (sku tshe brtan pa), the 'Free from Suffering Stupa' (mya ngan med), the 'Descent from Heaven Stupa' (lha babs), the 'Many Doors Stupa' (sgo mang), the 'Great Harmony Stupa' (dbyen sdum pa), the 'Magic Lotus Heap Stupa' (pad spungs cho 'phrul chen po), the 'Great Enlightenment Stupa' (byang chen) and the 'Complete Victory Stupa' (rnam rgyal); all these were built according to the method of the Kalachakra.

All the sponsors continually requested to be allowed to offer gilt umbrellas and fences made of gold, but he said: "If we do so, this umbrella will cause harm in bad times. So, instead, we shall use a big flat stone." Everyone was surprised and said that they would not be able to lift such a slab into place. They became very anxious, after which Buton Rinpoche relied on a magical formula through which he lifted a stone slab. The construction was then carried out with stone umbrellas made from big stone slabs decorated with a stone top ornament. On Thursday, the seventh day of the waxing moon of the 11th month, the first month of winter, in the conjunction of Bya gzug, the invocation ritual was performed and the flowers were scattered. After offering abundant offering substances of humans and gods, many wonderful signs were seen, such as rainbows and nets of grains of light.

Thus Buton Rinpoche acted in an excellent way as the glorious protector of all transmigrating beings and, by showing them (the path to happiness), he pleased many tens of thousands of people and satisfied all of them. He then performed the 'Mandala Ritual of Namgyalma, the Victor of the Three Realms' (khams gsum rnam rgyal), the 'Mandala Ritual of Mithrugpa' (mi 'khrugs pa), the 'Cremation of Corpses Ritual' (ro sreg), the 'Invocation of Yoga Tantra' (yoga'i rab gnas) and the 'Mandala Ritual of Amitayus, Destroyer of the Breath of the Lord of Death' ('chi bdag dbyug 'joms), as well as subsequent permissions to practice (rjes gnang) of both the peaceful and wrathful Vaisravana (nam sras) and the 'Elaborate Offering of Ritual Cakes'. By connecting many groups of people with the holy Dharma, amongst whom there was the great chief Wangchug Tsondru and others, he cultivated the seed of liberation for them.

In the year of the female water snake (1353), when he was 64 years old, the son in the sixth succession of the universal emperor Jengis Khan, Prince Prajnya Cing Zen Tsing Wang, together with 100 people from Mongolia requested the complete, profound and vast practices of the supreme Shri Kalachakra. Again he planted the seed of liberation for them and put an end to their cyclic existence. He installed faith in those who had none and, by increasing the faith of the faithful, he acted for the goal of many beings. As a gift of Dharma he was able to save the life of many prisoners who otherwise would have been executed.

At the orders of Lord Manjushri he wrote a 'Commentary on the Root Tantra of Shri Heruka', the 'Chö Jung' (chos 'byung), the 'Sa Cöd' (sa gcod), the 'Sadhana of Heruka' and a 'Short Scripture on the Mandala of Heruka' ('khrul 'khor gyi dpe chung) and the 'Mandala ritual of Heruka' (dkyil 'khor gyi cho ga). He then went to the big temple of Throphu Gaden (khro phu dga ldan) and occupied the seat of Throphu Lotsawa. He looked after the great philosophical and meditative schools and carried out the great deeds of the doctrine.

Then he went to the great monastery of the glorious Sakya, where he was invited by the exalted lineage masters of the stainless lineage of the glorious Sakyas, the great teacher Chökyi Gyaltsen Pal Zangpo and the teacher Lodrö Gyaltsen Pal Zangpo, who were great in family, lineage and attainment and he was highly honored there. He satisfied the protector of migrating beings, the Lord of Dharma, the unrivalled Sonam Gyaltsen Pal Zangpo, with the Dharma together with his nephew, as well as numerous learned, noble and excellent spiritual teachers of the mantra and philosophical schools of the great monastery, and countless other teachers of philosophy and Tantra who had gathered from here and there. The holders of the Tripitaka, altogether as many as the stars in the sky, were satisfied with the holy Dharma and he gave them many teachings, empowerments and instructions. Thus he acted extensively for the temporal and ultimate benefit of numerous people.

In the year of the male wooden horse (1354), when he was 65 years old, Buton Rinpoche stayed again at the precious monasteries of Zhalu and Riphug. Inwardly he meditated in single-pointed concentration on the meaning of the profound Meditation Buddha (thugs dam) while outwardly he attended to teachings, debate, composition and translation. He also completed the 'One Hundred Thousand Stories' (on violations of the rules of monastic discipline, 'dul ba gleng 'bum). At that time more than 160 spiritual teachers of philosophy and mantra and an assembly of more than 3,800 monks were staying in the great temple of Zhalu, and the Lord of Dharma stayed in their midst like a full moon mandala among the moving stars, as a glorious protector of all transmigrating beings and as a holy life-tree of the precious doctrine.

In the year of the female wood sheep (1355), when the Lord of Dharma was 66 years old, he went to the great monastery of Sakya again, where in the presence of the Lama of all transmigrating beings, Chökyi Gyaltsen Pal Zangpo, the successor of the glorious Sakya Pandita who was an emanation of Lord Manjushri himself, and who was unequalled in wisdom, compassion and enthusiastic perseverance, the Lord of Dharma erected a mandala of colored sand of the glorious supreme collection of the Dhyani Buddhas (dpal mchog rigs bsdus) 36 cubits wide and 108 cubits in circumference, after which he conferred the empowerment and gave the tantric teachings.

He also gave the empowerments and teachings of Yoga Tantra including Tsemo and Dorying (rtse mo, rdor dbyings), Namgyalma (khams gsum rnam rgyal), Kunrig, Ushnishavijaya (gtsug dgu), Vajrapani Conqueror of the Lord of Death (phyag rdor 'chi bdag 'joms pa), Chöying Sung Wang (chos dbyings gsung dbang), Yontan Kunjung (yon tan kun 'byung), Namkha Drime, Sangdan, Mitrugpa, Vajrasattva and so forth, as well as teachings on the root tantras and on all the commentaries.

The intention of this Lama was to spread the doctrine and make it flourish and to help the early friends of the doctrine obtain material support and stay healthy and by means of blessings to make all sentient beings comfortable and happy and especially benefit the practitioners of secret mantra, and above all to increase the meditation on Yoga Tantra. In return for the kindness of this great master and Abbot, the mandala of Shri Vajradhatu was constructed in the great temple, made from various precious substances with a root-line of 12 cubits of the forearm of the Lama himself. It was built as a square, inconceivable mansion with four corners and four entrances having four archways. In the middle of it was a square mandala with four corners and four entrances without archways. It had a golden vajra on top, and eight sides with precious jewels such as moon-crystals that radiated light.

Eight precious pillars on a golden circle supported four roofbeams adorned with painted decorations and surrounded by a round vajra construction. These vajras were all adorned with precious stones such as diamonds, lapis lazuli, crystal, emerald, turquoise, water-crystal, fire-crystal, nal(?) and yagod(?) and so forth. The roof was constructed in pagoda-style, with a full covering in two golden layers, like a royal palace. Outside there was a red platform all around with the objects of enjoyment for the senses, and in the space between the entrances and the hallways were precious jewels with radiating fire-crystals and golden vajras on top of them. On a golden moulding various strings of precious jewels were tied and suspended and, from the mouths of golden crocodiles on all sides, golden threads hung down from above and below with precious stones such as diamonds and lapis lazuli and so on tied with golden strings all spread out. They were suspended from jewel pillars with nets of pearls, half-nets of pearls and so forth. In the middle of the jewel nets there were large stones, ya-tail fans with bejewelled handles, various flowers and brocades, new moons, suns, jewels, mirrors and so on.

The pillars were set in precious vases and on top and at the base they were decorated with precious substances and in the middle with mirrors. The floor was made of blue lapis lazuli with silver white veins, and the golden balcony was ornamented with various precious substances. The archways consisted of various precious substances in 11 layers, on top of which there was a golden Dharma-wheel with a rim and a crystal hub, flanked by a golden male and female deer facing each other. In precious trees that grew from wish-granting vases there were silk hangings and bells in large and small nets, garlands of flowers and bundles of various brocades as well as garlands of precious jewels held by devas. The branches bent under the weight of the jewels and the flowers and, as they waved up and down, the clusters of ornamental golden bells resounded.

In short, it had all the characteristics of a complete, inconceivable mansion and in the middle was a golden throne supported by eight lions with a lotus and a moon disc, on top of which the great universal emperor Vairocana was seated. In the four directions were the four kings Akshobhya and so on in the fields. On the four sides of the great king there were the great queens such as Sattvi Vajrama. On the four sides of the four other kings were the 16 princes, such as Vajrasattva. In the inner corners were the four queens of the other kings, such as Gegmo, and in the four outer corners were the female servants such as Dugpöma, Solkhama, Ponyama and Branmo. At the four entrances there were the male servants, such as Chakyu and Solkha, Ponya and Bran.

The outer sphere was completely filled with the thousand great Buddhas of this fortunate era, Maitreya and so on. Apart from the devas mentioned already, at the four entrances there were special Aryas who possessed the quality of being very beneficial when seen, heard, remembered or touched.

It was erected from many precious substances including crystal, pearl, turquoise and coral as well as gold and conch shells and many medicinal scents such as sandal and duruka incense. Thus this inconceivable mansion was constructed of an excellent nature and perfect in design according to detailed instructions given by Buton Rinpoche who, in doing so, performed the vast deeds of the doctrine. He also wrote a text clarifying the arrangement of the inconceivable mansion and its ultimate nature.

This biography, called *A Handful of Flowers*, merely narrates some events which are like drops of water in the great ocean of good qualities that were achieved by the glorious holy master, the great scholar and translator Buton Rinpoche. It was written with faith and devotion on the 15th day of the first summer month in the year of the female wood sheep (1355) in the great monastery of the glorious Sakya, by the humble Rinchen Namgyal at the command of the second glorious Sakya Pandita Drung Chökyi Gyaltsen Pal Zangpo, after the seed of it had been written at the request of many spiritual friends including the lay vow holder, vajra holder and yogi of the highest vehicle Yong Drag Gyalpo (yongs grags rgyal po), who had perfect faith in this glorious master.

CHAPTER TWO

The time of Buton Rinpoche leaving Zhalu up to his death in 1364

Once the sheep year had passed, Buton spoke to the assembly of monks and laymen of Zhalu headed by the lords and the brothers: "I am getting old. I have been in charge of Zhalu Monastery for 37 years. Now I am no longer able to guide others, and it is the appropriate time for me to engage in the practices in preparation for death. If someone is put in charge of the monastery while I am still alive, there will be little chance of dispute later on. Please choose someone." To me he said, "It will be inappropriate if the seat is given to someone who is not a leading teacher."

They all asked him not to make such a request, to stay healthy and have a long life, saying: "Your Holiness' own teacher of philosophy, Tshad ma pa, kept on teaching until he was 83 years old, and he left his body while continuing to teach and explain the Dharma. Please do likewise."

Thus they repeated their requests again and again, but he replied that he could not go back on what he had said and that he was certain about his decision. He intended to engage himself completely in giving teachings in Riphug when the seat was occupied by someone else and, above all, he intended to engage in the practices. He said: "If you do not listen to this affectionate advice, you will regret it later. You should accept this message and just wait to see what happens. Even as I speak these words from my mouth, my life-tree shortens, so you should be clear about this.

"If I stay in the monastery, my mind will still go down to the caves and, while giving teachings, my body will tremble. I especially intend to engage in the practices now, while I can start without separating the father and children. I have gathered all the necessary things to be handed on in my residence and have sealed the door with bricks. I will go to the 'Lion's Cave' in Padro Tagtshang (spa dro stag tshang seng ge phug) and start the practice there." After deliberating upon all this they agreed with his decision to stay in Riphug.

So that he would not become displeased it was proper to choose someone to be the new Abbot. In line with the advice of the Lord of Dharma they requested the chief teacher Ngödrub Gyaltsen, but he did not consent. After that they requested the teacher Dharma Shri, but he also did not consent. Then I had to accept the seat, loading the burden of the *dzo* on to a goat. Virtually no one I know is the right person to be the head of the monastery. How can one be requested to occupy the seat of such a second Buddha? This is not a dream. I do not have the vast knowledge of the instructions concordant with the teachings of the all-knowing Arya, nor do I have the experience of meditation, a collection of disciples or wealth. Even the vows I guard have partly weakened. My mind is confused. My body and mind have but an ordinary appearance and have become clumsy and even my memory is like rolling down from a steep hill, unable to ascend again.

On the fifth day of the waxing moon of the first winter month in the year of the male fire monkey (1356), when the Lord of Dharma was 67 years old and wanted to devote himself to intensive practice, he entrusted the monastery to others. He wrote down instructions for the Abbot to act as a guide to others in conformity with the Dharma, and instructed the sponsor Kuzang Chenpo to look after the different kinds of students and assistants according to the Dharma. He also wrote down instructions for the Sangha-members about maintaining the doctrine of theory and practice in a correct manner.

He instructed the chief Rinchen Senge and so on to act as the principals of the noble people, and gave instructions for all the sponsors about the way to look after the doctrine, the Sangha community and the leaders, together with the groups of practitioners, and on how to protect the subjects, assistants and servants, the monks and the various laymen and so on, writing everything down in great detail. He then said: "Even if I do not die, this is still my good advice and, if I die, it is my testament, so you should take it seriously. Please do not lament and feel uncomfortable, and do not ask again for advice.

To me he gave a beautiful porcelain cup, a silver teapot and a hundred bushels of barley. He said: "This legacy is handed over as if these were old worn out things, so you may think that they are worthless. But when I first took over the residence, these were my only possessions. I had only 16 large and small religious implements, a following of 200 people, with seven or eight teachers of philosophy, and only one teacher, called Zhong Ddor (gzhong rdor), who was able to uphold mantra. You now have 1,000 followers, 100 Dharma teachers, many famous teachers of philosophy and mantra renowned in Central Tibet (dbus) and in Tsang, as well as many teachers of Tantra who are all able to be inner and outer vajra-teachers. This is what is given to you now and what you will be in charge of.

"In accordance with the time, the intelligent people will become fewer in number, it will become difficult to practice self-discipline and trouble is inevitable, but nourish yourself with the scriptural commentaries and try to gain complete understanding. By exerting yourself you will apprehend weariness and by being able to endure a great deal of hardship, you should look again at the testament I have written down for you. In this way you should do what is appropriate as well as you can. After some time there will be many who will come to you." Saying this, he left for Riphug.

On the way to Riphug the bell-maker Gonpo and a few others respectfully asked him whether he had handed over the monastery and he answered: "I have handed it over; I have no daughter to whom I have to give a dowry and the son is provided for." And everyone was content.

Then, in the fourth month of the year of the female fire bird (1357), the Pandit Sumana Shri arrived. From him he requested to complete the four empowerments in the mandala of Padmajala, the highest Avalokiteshvara (spyan ras gzigs bla med pad ma dra ba). He listened to the original Sanskrit texts of the sadhana, the mandala rituals, empowerment ritual, invocation and burnt offerings, all of which he translated into Tibetan. Although he said the Tantra texts would be delivered later, they were not. Furthermore, he translated the 'Tantra of the Bristling Riara' (ral pa gyen brdzes kyi rgyud) and the 'Commentary of Heruka' (bde mchog gi 'grel ba) by Tagpa Dorje (Tag pa'i rdo rje), as well as two short sadhanas of Heruka composed by Vibhuti.

Then he gave the complete teachings of Kalachakra, which he held to the second Sakya Pandita Chokyi Gyaltsen and to the Kashmiri Pandit Sumana Shri. Later, although he was no longer in charge of the monastery, he taught for nine years, passing on the complete teachings of Kalachakra to the great teacher Kunga Rinchen Gyaltsen Pal Zangpo Gushri, the great Jangchub Gyaltsen Tai Situ and Jampai Yang Sakya Gyaltsen Pal Zangpo. He also gave the 'Full Permission of Kalachakra' (dus 'khor yongs rdzogs gnang ba), the explanation of the extensive tantric commentary, the teaching on the 'Six Limbs of Preparatory Practice', together with the oral transmissions and the appropriate implements. Furthermore, he gave teachings on the 'Five Stages of Guhyasamaja' and the 'Shining Light of Yamantaka' (gshin rje gshes 'od gsal 'char ba) and so forth, teaching both the tantric practices and philosophy.

To the great Lama and Tishi Sonam Lodrö Gyaltsen Pal Zangpo (ti shri chen po bsod nams blo gros rgyal mtshan dpal bzang po) he gave the empowerments of the Vajramala (rdo rje 'phreng ba) and various subsequent permissions to practice (rje gnang) of Rigtä (rig gtad) and so on. To the Abbot Upadhyaya (gdan sa ba) and to the Acharya Dharmashri and Tshe'jam he gave the permission of Vajramala, as well as more teachings, empowerments and oral instructions in the four classes of tantra. In particular, to the great master Söloba (bsod blo ba) he gave the teachings on Yoga Tantra, and to Jamyangpa ('jam dbyangs pa) the permission of the 'Gloriously Supreme Tsemo' (dpal mchog rtse mo gnang ba), including the complete teachings on Yoga Tantra, such as 'The Training in the Final Practice' (sgrub pa rjes sgrub kyi phyag len bslab pa) of the Master Lha Khangpa.

At Kegnä (rkegs gnas), at the request of the Nyingmapa teacher Phagpa, he gave the extensive teachings on the 'Discernment of Valid Cognition' on one occasion, and later, at the request of the Abbot of the new Tsinä Namkha Rinchen (rtsis gnas gsar gyi mkhan po nam mkha' rin chen pa), one time he gave extensive teachings on the 'Abidharmasumuccaya'.

At the request of Jamyang Sakya Gyalba ('jam dbyangs sakya rgyal ba), he gave extensive teachings on the 'Sutra on Monastic Discipline'. Using all his time for the Dharma, in the autumn and in spring he gave extensive teachings on the 'Abhisamayalankara' and the oral transmissions (lung) of many of the Indian commentaries, together with the opinions stated by the many Tibetan spiritual teachers.

With his own hands Buton Rinpoche made faultless dharanis engraved in clay statues, that were placed in the numerous stupas he erected, which had perfect measurements and were consecrated by him with the invocation rituals.

With the general doctrine of Lord Buddha in mind and the great king and sponsor in particular, and above all the service for the holy master and Lord of Dharma Sonam Gyaltsen Pal Zangpo and his nephew, he inaugurated many mandalas, especially of the

Kalachakra and Vajradhatu, and established the custom of regular abundant offerings, which endured for a long period of time.

Then he put a lot of energy into the supervision of the erection of an assembly hall at Riphug, saying: "This is small and it would be better to make it larger." I asked him whether there was enough room for an assembly of more that 1,000, and whether that was sufficient. He said: "I am like the moon on the 29th day of the month. I will not stay long before dying, so you need to make offerings and assemble in prayer."

Once he was displeased with the words of a meditator who had come from Tsari and said: "When it is time to study philosophy he tries to become a meditator, and when it is time for meditation he is a philosopher. This is a very big error. It is not correct to engage in philosophical debate by merely wearing a worn-out cape and not enough for a meditator to merely be devoted to ashes. All of you should give teachings to the best of your ability; those who are unable to do so should keep their hands off philosophy. It is appropriate to attend exclusively to the preparatory practices of death. During my term as a teacher many practising teachers have died, and I imagine that I may also die in about seven years from now. So engage in the practice of meditation now!"

Earlier, when Buton Rinpoche was a student, he had many discussions with the teacher Lodrö Tshungme (blo gros mtshungs med) of Sangphu Nethog (gsang phu sne thog),[21] the karmic continuation of which continued to exist. Whereas the sutras which teach that all sentient beings possess a fully qualified Buddha potential require interpretation, according to the sutras which teach in a literal sense, the Buddha potential does not exist in a fully qualified manner in all beings. In accordance with the scriptures Buton Rinpoche now wrote a commentary called 'The Beautiful Ornament of the Tathagatagarbha' (bde gshes snying po mdzes rgyan).

In short, as for the earlier and later commentaries that he composed, he wrote: 'Meditations on the Mind of Enlightenment' (byang chub sems nyid sgom pa), 'Dedications for Those Who Have Died' (gshing po'i bsngo ba), 'The Accomplishment of the Purpose of the Four Persons' (skye bu bzhi'i don grub), 'A General Presentation of Monastic Discipline' ('dul ba syi'i rnam gzhag), 'Engaging in the Commentary of the Root-sutra' (mdo rtsa'i tika), the end of the 'Commentary on the Ritual Activities' (la chog gi tik), an 'Oral Instruction of the Past and the Future' (tshigs snya phyi'i gdams ngag), a 'Ritual to Benefit Householders' (khyim pa la phan gdags pa'i cho ga), a 'Commentary of Mothers' (ma rnam gyi 'grel ba), the 'Mandala Ritual of the Stainless Light' ('od zer dri med kyi dkyil chog), the 'Mandala Ritual of Avalokiteshvara Don Shag' (don zhags kyi dkyil chog), the 'Source of the Oral Transmission of Avalokiteshvara Don Shag' (lung khungs), 'A Medium Length Method to Accomplish Dharanis' (gzungs sgrub 'bring po), the 'Pacifying and Increasing Burnt Offering Rituals of Avalokiteshvara Don Shag' (don zhags zhi rgyas kyi sbyin sreg), the 'Increasing Burnt Offering Ritual of Vajradhatu' (rdo rje dbyings dbang rgyas kyi sbyin sreg), the 'Four Activities of the Training Tantra of Cudgelling (sbyon rgyud las bzhi'i brdun ba), the 'Glorious Supreme Final Practice' (dpal mchog sgrub pa rjes sgrub), a 'Praise of the Deities of the Mandala of Vajradhatu' (chos dbyings gsung dbang gi dkyil 'khor lha'i bstod pa), a 'Praise of Amitayus, Destroyer of the Lord of Death' (tshe dpag med 'chi bdag 'joms pa'i lha bstod pa), a 'Sadhana of the Lotus-like Avalokiteshvara' (thugs rje chen po pad ma dra ba'i sgrub thabs), a 'Melodious Dance of the Four Consecrations' (bka bsgo bzhi'i gar dbyangs), the 'Requests to the Lineage Gurus of the Final Instructions on the Five Stages' (rim lnga'i dmar khrid brgyud pa'i gsol 'debs), the 'Magic Circles of the Red, Black and Yamantaka Bhairava' (gshin rje gshes dmar nag 'jigs gsum gyi 'khrul 'khor), 'A Garland of Offerings to the Red, Black and Yamantaka Bhairava' (mchod phreng), 'Burnt Offering Rituals' (sbyin sreg), 'Ritual Cake Offerings' (gtor chog); the 'Mandala Practices of the Thirteen Red Bhairavas' (gshed dmar bcu gsum ma'i sgrub dkyil), the 'Mandala ritual of Yamantaka in the Tradition of the Translator Ra' ('jigs byed rva lugs kyi dkyil chog), the 'Ritual Cake Offering to Kalarupa' (las gshin gyi gtor chog), the 'Practice of the Feast of the Heroes in Tantric Offering Ceremonies' (tshogs 'khor dang dpa'i bo;i ston mo'i lag len), 'Body Isolation' (lus sbyon), 'Magic Circles' (khrul 'khor), the 'Practice of Heruka in the Luipa Tradition' (bde mchog lu'i pa'i sgrub dkyil), the 'Burnt Offerings' (sbyin sreg), 'A Garland of Offerings' (mchod phreng), 'The Dance of the Goddesses with the Offerings' (nyer spyod dang lha mo'i gar), a 'Commentary to the Sadhana of Nagpopa' (nag po pa'i sgrub thabs kyi 'grel pa), the 'Sadhana of Nagpopa' (nag po pa'i sgrub thabs), the 'Mandala Practice of Ganthapada' (dril bu pa'i sgrub dkyil), the 'Commentary of the Practice of all Dakinis' (mkha' 'gro kun spyod kyi tika), 'The Twenty Offerings of the Four Places', 'A Presentation of Gola' (gdan bzhi'i mchod pa nyi shu), 'The Mandala of the Sun for Each Day' (nyin zhag re la nyi ma'i kyil 'khor), and 'The Counting of the Suns' Declinations (gdung byed kyis bgrod pa'i tshad), the 'Quick Astrological Method for the Five Planets' (gza' lnga myur rtsis kyi lhan thabs), the 'Kalachakra Mantra' (dus 'khor gyi sngags), the 'Sixteen Limbs' (rkang pa bcu drug pa), the 'Seventy-Two Limbs' (rkang pa bdun cu rtsa gnyis pa), the 'Dance of the Kisses' (sbyar ba'i gar), the 'Seven Main Limbs' (rtsa ba'i rkang stabs bdun), 'The Dance of the Twelve Goddesses of Kalachakra' (dus 'khor lha mo bcu gnyis kyi gar), and the 'Words of the Mantra of the Ritual Cake' (gtor snags tshigs bcad du bsgyur ba), the 'Highest Empowerment' (dbang gong ma), the 'Ritual Offerings to the Thirty-Six Yoginis' (rnal 'byor ma so drug gi mchod chog), the 'Requests to the Lineage of Ladrö' (rva 'bro brgyud pa'i gsol 'debs), 'The Way to Arrange the Deities of the Outer Circle of Kalachakra' (dus 'khor khor yug gi lha 'god tshul), 'Answers' (dris lam) to the 'Questions of the Great Acharya Chökyi Gyaltsen, Sonam Lodrö Gyaltsen, Müpa Deleg Zangpo, Samdrub Wangyal (chos kyi rgyal mtshan, bsod nams blo gros rgyal mtshan, mus pa bde legs bzang po, bsam grub dpal rgyal) and others' as well as the 'Fifteen Holy Mahayana Practices' (gdams pa'i chos chen po bco lnga) to Minyag Loden (mi nyag blo ldan).

After writing all these works, he went to the 'Source of the Deep Practices of Ebo' (ebo dong chos kyi 'byung gnas), where he conferred the invocation rituals of the great temple and met with the Lords of Dharma, uncle and nephew and with Prince Thogmed and others and gave them the instructions they required.

Next he went to the Springs of Palgyi Dechen (chu mig dpal gyi sde chen) where he met with the envoy of the Mongols, the uncle and nephew and the masters, the great Tai Situ and others, and the edict of the Mongols was proclaimed.

He was invited to Tagtsal Dzing (stag tshal rdzin kha) by the chief Rinchen Pal Zangpo and he supervised the invocation of numerous sutra texts written in gold. Then he went to Rinchen Pungpa (rin chen spungs pa) where he gave teachings on philosophy, on monastic discipline and on Tantra, including the Kalachakra Tantra. Afterwards, Nangchen Phagpa invited him to Nyangtö Cangra (nyang stod lcang ra), where he conferred the invocation rituals on many texts that had been written in gold.

When he performed the ritual of the generation of the mind of enlightenment according to the Madhyamika tradition, he completely satisfied the great scholars Nä Nyingpa and Nangchenpa (gnas rnying pa dang nang chen pa) and others with the practices of the Mahayana. He acted in such a way that those who had not yet obtained the Bodhisattva vow obtained it, and those who had obtained it but let it deteriorate, restored it. In this way he worked for the well-being of countless transmigrating beings.

Furthermore, he went to Tagtshang Dzongkha, Zhudrognä and Shangthong Mön (stag tshang rdzongkha, zhu 'brog gnas, sangs mthong mon), where he ripened many people and put them on the path to liberation. Then he stayed again at the precious monastery of Riphug. He was inwardly engaged in pure concentration, while outwardly he preserved the doctrine by giving teachings.

From the three regions of Naris (mnga ris skor gsum), from the three heights of Kham (mdo khams sgang gsum) and from the four regions of Central Tibet (dbus) and Tsang, many intelligent people intent on hearing, contemplating and meditating came for an audience with him and he exerted himself day and night in the study and practice of the Dharma, of scriptures and realizations. At that time he decided to completely give up all possessions. He called me, saying "Come while I am here in Zhalu." When I came to him he said: "All the spiritual teachers of Central Tibet and Tsang who were my contemporaries have died. All my debating partners from the time of my studies except for Zhang Dyapepa (zhang bya dpe ba) are no longer here, and I shall soon die too. After I have died, I do not know what my root of virtue will bring about, as my root of virtue will precede me. I will bid farewell in the morning and go to Tushita, so you must come tonight."

Completely abandoning avarice and attachment, he gave me a good garment, saying: "Wear it until it is worn out; be resolute as it will be necessary." This I understood to be his teaching by intimation. At that time, beneath the overhead balcony, the disciple Drag Zong (grags gzhong) asked if the renunciation was definite and the master answered: "In truth it is definite, this is my farewell before going to Tushita."

When he performed the earth ritual (sa chog) of Kalachakra and preparations for the full moon day in the temple, he was tired. The master Dor Zhongpa (rdor gzhong pa) and many others assembled and the full Kalachakra practices were performed. Then he said that he wished to go into the presence of Maitreyanatha and that they should gather the next day. The others remained silent but Latöpa Logya bowed down and said: "Please do not do so. In Tushita, Maitreya himself teaches the Dharma. I beseech you to stay here." But he did not reply.

Once when he was seated in the courtyard at Riphug in the midst of many pupils who had assembled there and an assistant monk was massaging his feet, the Lord of Dharma said: "Last night I had an auspicious dream. There were three long staircases stretching down from Tushita. Maitreya descended the central one, and on one side he ascended again and asked who would come along on the other side. At that time it was established that I would surely go to Tushita."

During the summer term of the year of the ox (1361), I considered that I had conceived a strong thought motivated by the three poisons of hatred, greed and ignorance. Without mentioning it to anyone, I went to Riphug for the autumn term. When the 'Abhisamayalankara' was taught he looked at me with wide open eyes for a moment and said that sometimes thoughts are wrong ideas and it is not good to foster them. If one does so it is as terrifying as the head of a calf becoming a yak. His Holiness expressed exactly what was in my mind and I became afraid of this. There were many such inconceivable instances of his clairvoyance of the thoughts of others through direct bare perception.

In the fifth month of the year of the male water tiger (1362), the assistant monks Nyenä Gelong and Jampal were drawing a chart with the intervals of the conjunctions of the constellations of the five main planets (thun zhor la lnga bsdus kyi rimo), and he saw this while he was taking a walk.

Since, according to the teachings and views of Kalachakra, there is no way to exclude even one of these planets, he said: "You should first learn this properly. When one makes charts merely knowing the outer measurements, there will be occasions where trifling mistakes like these arise which contradict the conjunctions and the charts will then not correspond with the visible conjunctions. Only fools proclaim the time of certain conjunctions they do not understand, and they will experience hindrances. Even when the teacher Nagarjuna was still young he was able to calculate every day of that period, while others were still searching for a method. When an astrological chart is made without taking into account the connection of the year with the months, nobody can use it as a support. In the future many charts will be wasted and remain misunderstood.

"When a round hole lies in a circumscribed space, one may expect to meet with a big obstacle. One may think that one will experience an obstacle in obtaining a certain level of meditation, whereas the chart does not correspond to the visible constellations. One may think about reasons for this and make a lot of false predictions. One may become afraid and in this way one will not come to understand the true mode of existence of phenomena. If charts are made in this way, this kind of wrong understanding will be the outcome and even when one asks someone else with a lot of faith, unless they are all-knowing they will not know. Therefore, make prostrations and get started. The way it appears to me in your chart, there are about seven years to go to the last month of the year of the female earth bird, so you should examine whether this is correct or not. If you do not figure this out now while I am here, you may never come to know it, as I will die soon. There will be nobody else whom you can ask and you and your charts will not be trustworthy. You will find yourself not knowing what to say.

"Because you think that there may be obstacles, you will make many more charts and you will still not find any changes for the worse or the better. You may never be able to draw other than such wrong charts. You may claim to have found the bird year, but when we investigate well, we find the 15th day of the last month in the female earth bird. Any mandalas derived from this chart will be wasted. You should use the seventh branch of the moving elements when from the beginning of the first lunar mansion (bra nye) you get the appearance of 39 hours and 18 chusang (chu srang) and look at the outcome of this. Why is this so? The stars are in the first lunar mansion. If you merely say that the hours and the chusang are this and that, even though it may be correct, you continue to fail to understand why it is correct. You simply won't know. In this situation you should draw an expanded chart and, if you do so, it will contain the inherent meaning." By giving this answer, the visual constellations above the 25th lunar constellation were completely investigated, but for the 20 hours and 42 chusang. He then wrote down tables for quick calculation and said: "Now you will know it, even if I die now."

Furthermore, on one side of the assembly hall he clearly outlined the correlation of the regions of the world, measuring 400,000 yoyonas (pagtsé) from the outer atmosphere up to the central mountain and the hot hells. By applying pure measurements such as the four cubits of a body he revealed many other hidden things which became clear and recitations were made easy to understand, but there is no time to go into these now.

It was also necessary to revise the texts on Sutra and Tantra and to compile a manual. He said that they should be finished, for if he died beforehand, learned and earnest scholars and monks would look at them and deride them, saying that not even one person revised these texts. And if an ignorant person were to look at them, he would proceed hastily and quickly become arrogant.

He said that when some people said to Ananda, "Ananda, a person suffering from old age loses his memory and, while he does not remember things well, his mind is troubled by his ageing," Ananda became sad and said: "The elders have already passed away and the young are not like me; I remain in meditation like a solitary bird. As all my friends and relatives have already departed, there is no spiritual teacher here who remembers dwelling on the levels of meditation." Buton Rinpoche said this with the intention and the thought to inspire others. He looked with great compassion at the assistants and monks and he said: "In such a year I completed my studies. In such a year I acted as the Abbot of Zhalu. Not all of you are young, but there are many young people here. Some of you have become novices, yet do not know the Vinaya. Some of you have become fully ordained monks, but do not know the Vinaya rituals. Although some of you claim to be tantric practitioners, you do not know about the 'Fifty Verses of Devotion for the Spiritual Master' (bla ma lnga bcu pa) and about the 'Fourteen Root-transgressions of the Tantric Vow' (rtsa ltung bcu bzhi pa).[22] Is this armor not becoming lighter? Is there nothing that needs to be done? Is this sufficient?"

In this way he gave advice to all the Sangha-members. To all the tantric practitioners he said: "You who are followers of the old tradition of mantra (nying ma pa), the best of you must learn the 'Abhidharmasamuccaya' and the 'Discernment of Valid Cognition' and the lesser ones are to learn merely parts of the Abhidharma and Valid Cognition. All the tantrikas of today belonging to the old and new traditions need to be able to differentiate between the respective tantric commentaries of the contemporary old and new tantric traditions." He said all this to inspire them.

To me he said: "It is embarrassing to be called a translator if one has not translated anything. First translate the 'Practices to Become Omniscient' (thams cad mkhyen pa grub pa) and concentrate on grammar. If you can find a pandit, you should think of revising the 'Commentary on the Terms' (sgra'i tika) ,the 'Removal of the Ascending Hair-tuft' (ral pa gyen brdzes). If you do not find such a pandit you can revise the 'Twenty Mandala Rituals' (dkyil mchog nyi shu pa) and the 'Presentation of the Five Stages of Guhyasamaja'. If someone were to argue that there is no need for this, since there is nobody who practices it, you should understand that such a statement is like a prophecy that it will become extinct."

By the end of the winter of the year of the female water hare (1363) I went to Zhalu. Students were arriving for the winter courses and meditators were to take the retreat commitment. The time had come to engage solely in virtuous practice, and the practitioners were to engage in isolated retreat in closed cells. He said: "O monks, you should exert yourselves in the complete practices of Kalachakra. As for me, since I myself have grown old now, my thirst has diminished; since you are busy, while it is warm give up serving tea; you should serve three tea (breaks) in the cell." Holding his body in the meditation posture, he took his evening tea in the cell, and when it was warm he took a walk. In the evening he performed the full practices of Heruka in the Luipa tradition together with the self-empowerment. Except for these activities, he remained constantly in a sitting posture at all times, day and night, and did not put his head on a pillow, engaging solely in the practice of meditation.

At the beginning of the first day of the second month in the year of the male wood dragon (1364), he started getting ill. On the 15th there was an eclipse of the moon, and with the new moon there was also an eclipse of the sun, which turned dark red and gave out no light. Several bad omen like these occurred. Under the leadership of Prince Thogmed, many Sangha-members and sponsors offered golden mandalas and made single-pointed requests. Just as Maudgalyayana showed the aspect of good health in order to save the physician from punishment, so the Lord of Dharma saw several advantages and disadvantages and showed the aspect of an improvement of his health starting from the 16th day of the middle spring month.

He said: "Last night I had a dream in which the Dharma Protectors removed my sickness and covered my body with many shields of armor. As the Dharma Protectors have benefited me in this way, we should carefully conduct a thanksgiving offering to them on the eighth day of the next month. I will see to it that we start the preparations for the ritual cake offerings and the other offerings."

As he was physically healthy again on the eighth day of the last spring month, the ritual cakes were offered to the Dharma Protectors and he made as many as 40 circumambulations. He said that he felt even more comfortable than when he was a student.

He then stopped his retreat and ordered the performance of elaborate practices, but they asked him not to end the retreat. Those around him performed the elaborate practices in the assembly hall, while in his own room the Lord of Dharma performed the practices of Guhyasamaja Akshobhya Vajra (gsang 'dus mi bskyod rdo rje), after which the 10 directions were filled with reports of his sparkling health.

On the first day of the waning moon of the first summer month he showed the aspect of falling ill again. Because he had attained the unchanging vajra-body of Akshobhya, he was no longer subject to illness, but as it is stated in the Gyu Lama (Uttara Tantra):

> "Even though, because of pure insight, he is beyond birth and so on, the Great Compassionate One shows the aspect of birth, old age, sickness and death, so that ordinary beings may see the state of purity".

As stated here, Buton Rinpoche showed the aspect of being ill through various means, and great masters and wise physicians such as Kyor Lungpa were consulted. Extensive ceremonies were performed, such as practices of and offerings to the Meditation Buddhas, recitations of the sacred texts and offerings to the Sangha-members. Although there were two monks and two spiritual teachers in his presence constantly, who exerted themselves in serving him all the time, in order to train all impure students and to show that the ways of karma are inconceivable, he did not recover physically again.

At that time his great disciple Tonpa (ston pa) asked for his patron's advice, saying: "I am confused about this." He thought that if they had listened, they would have many things to attend to, but if they had not, things might not get done properly, but he said nothing. Previously he had ordered the monks to prepare enough food and drink for a long time. To me he said: "Take some yourself, it is good to take a portion equal to mine." Those were his last words to me. And these were indeed his final words, as the assistant Gelong Dondrub reported.

On the 20th day of that month he stopped speaking and never spoke again. In the seventh month of the year of the female terrific spirit (1364), when 3,497(?) years of the Buddhist doctrine had passed and the Lord of Dharma was 75 years old, that is early in the morning of the 21st day of the sixth month of the year of the male wood dragon, with the sun in the house of Cancer and the moon in the first constellation Ashrini (tha skar), when all the conjunctions (favorable to) wholesome activity, the good signs of the astrological charts coincided and the time of the conjunction of the ox was rising, Buton Rinpoche showed the aspect of his passing into the sphere of the peaceful Dharmakaya.

On the 27th the remains were purified. For one month the chamber with the remains was left untouched, while many students, disciples, sponsors and spiritual teachers gathered to perform the offering ceremonies for the remains. After one month the chamber with the remains was opened and the remains and relics were distributed in all directions, down to India, up to China and to all the regions of Nepal and Tibet.

The great supreme Mongol King and his son, the Lord of the doctrine and Lord of the Dharma Sonam Gyaltsen Pal Zangpo and his nephew headed the large gatherings of great and small, high and low, supreme, mediocre and small-scope disciples to worship this basis of reverence. Especially in the great temple of the glorious Zhalu, a wonderful inner monument was made as large as the physical size of the Jowo Rinpoche, while the outer monument was made in the shape of a golden stupa, a 'Great Harmony Stupa' (dbyen sdum pa'i mchod rten).

In the precious monastery of Riphug an image was constructed which bore such a close resemblance that it seemed real, along with a holy object containing the essence off the relic pills and the remains. After that many great disciples and spiritual teachers conferred extensive and pure consecration rituals (rab gnas) and ceremonies to the satisfaction of everyone.

At the time when all these were performed, there were signs such as earth-shocks, lights and thunder, and the atmosphere was filled with rainbows. Some of these rainbows were like five-colored tent roofs, some were like draped curtains, some like rainbow canopies, umbrellas, suspended banners, spread out peacock feathers and canopies of glossy silk cloth, and some were like skilful divinely-drawn lotuses; there were so many variants that it is impossible to recount them all.

An inner 'great enlightenment stupa' was made at Riphug. When it was taken to Zhalu and when during the consecration rituals the flowers were scattered, the devas caused a rain of flowers to fall. Although his appearance had been ordinary, it was clear to everyone that Buton Rinpoche had in fact obtained great realizations.

They performed the prayers, fulfilling the wishes of the deceased, and the various mandala meditations. Principally the great mandala practices of the complete Body, Speech and Mind mandalas of Shri Kalachakra and the great mandala of Shri Vajradhatu were extensively performed. The offerings of the Eight Tathagatas were conducted many times form the 27th onwards up to the 18th, for 21 days. Outer and inner practices were performed 1,538 times and concluded with the burnt offerings.

The practices of the Medicine Buddhas were performed 6,300 times and the complete Kagyur was recited three times. In all the temples big lamps were offered and offerings were made to the Sangha-members. Many tsok-offerings and tea-offerings were performed as well as offerings of ritual cakes to please the Dharma Protectors and ghosts.

Especially and in complete accordance with Buton Rinpoche's wishes concerning his departing, offerings of food and tea were made to the monks many times in all the large and small monasteries, with the great monastery of the glorious Sakya as the main one, and in the four divisions of the Jogdan (jo gdan). On the early morning of the 24th an offering of tea and food was made together with a distribution to 200 monks, mainly from the two monasteries of Zhalu, and at the proper time the extensive practices were done during the annual offering ceremony, and these included the presentation of gifts to many lay people and to the monks of the two monasteries.

At the great monthly offering-assembly, food and tea were offered to the assembly and the offering practices and practices of the Medicine Buddhas were performed every month for one year. From then onwards, at each monthly tea offering, the pupils and sponsors including his Holiness the Lord of Dharma offered tea to the assembly and so forth, along with great masters such as the great Tai Situ and his nephew, the great chief Namkha Tenpai Gyaltsen Pal Zangpo (nam mkha'i bstan pa'i rgyal mtshan) and the great Enshawa (sku zhang du dben shva), and others besides.

The great disciple Tonpa (ston pa) carried out the wishes of the Lord of Dharma in full, bearing wealth, loss and difficulty, supported by faithful students and sponsors. Particularly the abbots and preceptors and the spiritual teachers together with the other Sangha-members conducted extensive teachings and practices without any laziness, and thus they carried out in full the wishes of the Lord of Dharma.

When even the All-knowing Ones do not venture to express the quality and quantity of his great deeds, how could this be the object of activity of confused fools like myself? However, faults do not arise within a virtuous mind. Therefore even a small part of this boundless and wonderful flower garland biography of this great master is precious in the hands of the faithful. I pray that the great Lord of Dharma may always care for us with his great compassion.

Concluding prayer

I bow down at the feet of the Master, Buton Rinpoche,
You who eradicates the darkness from the minds of beings
By radiating boundless light rays from the fully evolved
mandala of wisdom and compassion;
And you who enacts boundless enlightened activities,
Guiding them by the chariot of the two collections.

I bow down at the feet of the great translator Buton Rinpoche,
You, the Lord of Dharma, who always performs
The four kinds of enlightened activities[23]
From the three precious Bodies (kayas),
Which you manifested as the result of thorough training
In the two collections during boundless eons.

I bow down to you who attained the peace of the Dharmakaya,
And realized the individual potential of yourself
In the sphere and cognition of non-duality,
Which is beyond birth and death and conceives of nothing;
And whose nature, pure from the beginning,
Is spontaneously accomplished.

I bow down to you who possesses
The completion of the Yuganadha,
Which is the uncommon practice of
Inseparable bliss and emptiness;
From which you actually discipline
The pure objects to be disciplined (Aryas)
With your (Sambhogakaya) body of a great person,
Not subject to birth and death.

I bow down to you who reveals manifold emanations
Of Nirmanakayas from your practice
Of inseparable emptiness and appearance to
Discipline the various groups of impure and pure objects
To be disciplined throughout the extent of space.

I bow down to you who realized that, from the beginning,
Phenomena are without origination and cessation,
And freed yourself from the bonds of birth and death;

Who, conforming with the notions of objects to be tamed,
Showed the aspect of taking birth, training
In all the sciences and arts such as writing.

I bow down to you who obtained power over
Interdependent relations with manifold methods,
And actually made no distinction between self and others;
Who attained the realization of the one taste
Of inseparable samsara and nirvana,
Yet still vanquishes the groups of demons
With the power of having attained perfection
In the generation and completion stages.

I bow down to you, the all-knowing one,
The great pandit of the five sciences.
You had completely mastered all the sciences,
Yet showed the aspect of a student and trained in grammar,
Logic, art, medicine and, above all,
In the science of mind (Buddhism).

I bow down to you who had thoroughly given up
The objects of abandonment, and had already gained perfection
In the training of all the precepts, yet still practiced
The teachings of the five classes of vows
For individual liberation, in order to look after the doctrine
And preserve it for the future.

I bow down to you who had given up
The stains of the three doors
And had gained perfection in the results of the paths and stages,
Yet still relied on various tutoring masters, and fully conducted
The transmissions and empowerments of tantra.

I bow down to you who directly perceived
The one taste of great bliss and emptiness
In the experience of the ultimate state of Yuganadha;
Through the doors of single-pointed concentration and
By the force of the powers you did not even rest
In the post-meditation periods,
But were always absorbed in meditative concentration.

I bow down to you who are an unrivalled friend
Of all sentient beings, who engages in
Relative and ultimate reality simultaneously

And, equalizing yourself with others, cherishes others
More than yourself and possesses the mind of enlightenment.

I bow down to you who have crossed an ocean of practices,
And have acquired expertise in establishing, refuting and so on,
And, solely considering to benefit others by the scriptures
And realizations of the Three Vehicles,
Engaged in analyses, debate and writing.

I bow down to you who, even though you had already
Overcome the bondage of birth and death,
Showed birth and death for the sake of others,
And for the sake of those to be disciplined,
Including myself, who still hold things to be permanent,
Showed the way of passing from this world.

I bow down to you who gained perfection in liberating others;
Even when your physical elements stopped functioning,
Your continuum never ceased the enlightened activities of
Disciplining beings through a variety of methods,
With your remains, your relics and your written words.

I bow down to you, the master who obtained the power of
Emanations, and although you showed your passing beyond
To the sphere of peace, you show a variety
Of inconceivable supreme and other emanations
To subdue the objects to be disciplined.

I bow down to you who, for countless eons, familiarized yourself
With meritorious activities and exerted yourself in respect, love
And humility, and therefore you possess all good qualities of
Generosity and the other perfections, and your mind and
Secret speech are blessed with power and capacity.

I bow down to you who was never displeased with offerings
When you were the object of veneration,
But were skilful in power and wisdom and of venerable descent;
Although you were renowned for your renunciation and ethics
And were very learned in these,
You were always free from arrogance.

I bow down to you who have the power of
Countless good qualities such as compassion,
The extraordinary resolve, generosity and discipline,

And exert yourself in benefiting others
In concordance with your vows, you who are disciplined
In your senses and have the appearance of a hero.

I bow down to you who are adorned with stainless ethics;
Whose activities of body, speech and mind are well disciplined,
And whose behavior is totally non-violent towards others;
Thus you are adorned with stainless ethics,
Well disciplined and calm.

I bow down to you who adheres closely
To the theory and practice of the Dharma,
Who knows both the literal and interpretative meanings,
The words and the meaning, and possesses
Generosity, gentle words and clear analyses,
And who strives for the common interest,
The meaning of the Dharma
And the literal words and presence of mind.

You have an unobscured and crystal-clear knowledge
Of the three times.
Children who lament, their eyes filled with tears,
Being weary of unbearable confusion,
Look around to see who, other than yourself,
Is a repose of their hopes.

You went to another place where the Lords of Dharma
Shine with thousands of lights;
You have set the demons of false speech apart,
Whereas we wander in the gloom of ignorance, saying:
"Alas, we do not know what to do!"

The firewood of the heart is consumed by the fire of suffering;
Although you cry with sorrow, we are tired from weeping
And our minds capable; like chopped wood,
Our bodies are flung to the ground.
Can you, in your compassion, bear such a plight?

You have the power of mind of the complete doctrine,
And we wish to uphold the doctrine;
You who have the power have proceeded to the happy realm.
What are we powerless ones to do now?

Please, our only father, come back to this place once more,
And look after us fortunate ones.

May the remains of the doctrine not become
Like a fading butterlamp in mid-air,
But may we also in all our lives be adorned with
The glory of a conducive body and good qualities;
Having trained well in the points of
Hearing, contemplating and meditating,
May we effortlessly perform the purpose of others.

May we in all our lives follow you as closely as your shadow,
And, after devoting ourselves respectfully
To the dust particles of your feet,
May we drink from the essential nectar of your teachings,
And come to hold the secret treasure
Of your body, speech and mind?

When you, O Lord of Dharma, manifest Buddhahood
Under the tree of enlightenment,
May I take birth beneath your principal disciples and,
During one of your discourses, obtain the supreme prophecy
That I may become a glorious protector
Of transmigrating beings like yourself.

May I, at the time of death and changing my body,
Be born in Tushita as a divine child at your feet,
And, having been born with a body to practice the Mahayana,
May I obtain stability in the practice of non-origination.

May I, from then onwards until I attain enlightenment,
Never be born as a human without power of richness,
But have the power to take birth wherever I can benefit others,
And engage in the great waves of the Bodhisattva practices.

May I become a ferryman who liberates countless beings
From the raging waves of samsara's depths
And profound sufferings, with its mischievous demons
Of birth, ageing, sickness and death,
And free them from the inexhaustible disturbing emotions
Of the ocean of worldly existence so difficult to cross.

This concludes the biography entitled "A Handful of Flowers", which narrates the lifestory of the glorious master Buton Rinchen Drub, Lord of Zhalu. It was written down by Gelong Dratshadpa with the assistance of the bhikshu and spiritual friend Sonam Drub (bsod nams drub), at the request of many close disciples and sponsors of the precious Lord of Dharma on the 21st day of the last month of spring in the year of the female fire horse (1366) in the monastic hermitage of Riphug.

May the great ocean of samsaric suffering hereby soon dry up!

Shubam

These words were printed after Gelong Tangyan (bstan rgyan) offered money and made requests at the great Lama's household of Gyaltsen Thonpa (rgyal mtshan mthon pa). The positive energy of this is completely dedicated towards enlightenment.

This inspiring biography of the great translator Buton Rinpoche was translated from the Tibetan by Hans van den Bogaert at the request of Noortje Toetenel, who is a true Mother of all children. The first half of the draft translation was corrected with the kind assistance of the Venerable Geshe Sonam Gyaltsen, resident teacher at the Maitreya Institute in Holland, and the second half was checked with a translation of D.S. Ruegg to which the great Master Dapo Rinpoche Jampa Gyatso from Paris had generously contributed from his great ocean of wisdom.

NOTES

1. Twelve Stages (Sa bcu gnyis). These are the ten stages of a Bodhisattva plus the stage prior to generating the mind of enlightenment (byang chub to sems ma bskyed pa'i sa) and the ever-illuminating ground (kun tu 'od kyi sa).
2. Corpus of Complete Enjoyment (Skt: Sambhogakaya. Tib: longs spyod rdzogs pa'i sku). That form of a Buddha which is accessible only to Arya Bodhisattvas. A Sambhogakaya form of Buddha is adorned with five qualities: 1. He resides only in Akanista heaven 2. He lives until the end of Samsara 3. He is adorned with the 32 major and 80 minor marks of a Buddha. 4. He is always surrounded by disciples of Bodhisattvas on the tenth stage. 5. He preaches only Mahayana doctrine.
3. Corpora of Emanation (Skt: Nirmanakaya. Tib: sprul sku). That form of a Buddha rooted in the Sambhogakaya aspect of Buddhas which appears in different forms in the samsaric realm; these forms are accessible to all kinds of beings. Such Buddhas may come in three different forms: as artisans; as a living or non-living phenomenon; and as a monk.
4. Vajrasana (Buddhagaya/rdo rje gdan). The holiest place of Buddhist pilgrimage in the state of Bihar in India, where the present Buddha Shakyamuni achieved his complete enlightenment. For Mahayanists this is the place where the Buddhas of all the three times would also attain their complete enlightenment.
5. Chakravarti king ('khor los sgyur ba'i rgyal po). The universal monarchs in Buddhist legend. It is believed that these kings only appeared during the period when the lifespan of human beings ranged from 80,000 years to infinity. It is believed that the lifespan of contemporary human beings is only 100 years, and such kings do not appear any more.
6. Shravaka (nyan thos). The practitioners of one of the three Vehicles who do not believe in the interpretative aspects of teachings of the Mahayana Vehicle. Philosophically they assert and believe in the existence of only gross selflessness and not subtle selflessness. The meditation on Shamatha and Vipasyana is very popular among the followers of this particular Vehicle. There are 18 sub-schools within the Shravakas.
7. Pratekya Buddha (rang sangs rgyas). Arhats who do not rely on teachers during the last phase of their life but contemplate

the principles of dependently arising phenomena and achieve Arhatship through partial realization of the selflessness of person and selflessness of phenomena.

8. Abhisamayalankara (mngon rtogs rgyan). One of the five principal texts of Indian Buddhist philosophy studied in the major monastic universities of Tibet. The text deals with eight topics of paths to Buddhahood, primarily about the method aspects. The text is authored by Maitreya.
9. Vikramapuri. Vikramalashila, the famous ancient Indian Buddhist centre of learning at Magadha founded by king Dharmapala on the banks of the Ganges. Atisha was the chief priest of this monastic university before he left for Tibet. It was destroyed during the Mughal period in the 11th century.
10. Odantapuri. A famous Indian temple built by Acharya Simha Bhadra under the patronage of Dharmaraja Dharmapala. It was used as the model by Acharya Shanta Rakshita for Tibet's first monastic centre of learning, Samye, during the 9th century.
11. Sems sde ma bu bco brgyad. The 18 texts of Dzogchen tantras popular in the Nyingma tradition, translated by Vairochana, Vimalamitra, Kumaraja and Yudra Nyingpo. See: *Tibetan English Dictionary of Buddhist Terminology*, Tsepak Rigzin, LTWA 1993, pp. 284-285
12. The extensive, medium and short Perfection of Wisdom Sutras (yum rgyas 'bring bsdus gsum). The extensive version of the Wisdom Sutra text comprises 100,000 verses; the medium version comprises 25,000 verses and the short version comprises 8,000 verses only. These form a portion of the Buddhist canon.
13. Five great stages (sa sde lnga), Five Treatises of Asanga which are: 1. Grounds of Yogic Practices (Yogacharyabhumi); 2. Compendium of Ascertainment (Nirnayasamgraha); 3. Compendium of Bases (Vastusamgraha); 4. Compendium of Enumerators (Paryayasamgraha); 5. Compendium of Explanation (Vivaranasamgraha).
14. Prakarana sde brgyad. The eight treatises of Vasubandhu. See: *Tibetan English Dictionary of Buddhist Terminology*, Tsepak Rigzin, LTWA 1993, pp. 164.
15. Yoga with and without signs (mtsan bcas mtsan med kyi rnal 'byor). A meditation practice in the lower tantras, in which in the former (ie. yoga with signs) a meditator visualizes and meditates on his meditational deity in close proximity to a close relation or friend; while in the latter (ie. yoga without signs) a

meditator primarily meditates on the ultimate mind of enlightenment during the three stages of the engagement, abidance and awakening distinctly.

16. Six Yogas of Naropa (na ro chos drug): 1. Yoga of psychic heat; 2. Yoga of clear light; 3. Yoga of illusory body; 4. Yoga of intermediate rebirth; 5. Yoga of consciousness transference; and 6. Yoga of entering a corpse.
17. Sbyor ba yan lag drug gi gdams pa. The six yogas of wind meditation according to Kalachakra tantra: 1. Yoga of withdrawal; 2. Yoga of concentration; 3. Yoga of pinpointing the life-sustaining wind; 4. Yoga of retention; 5. Yoga of recollections; and 6. Yoga of single-pointed concentration.
18. Zhva lu ser khang. A monastic institution located in the district of Zhi Kha Tse in central Tibet. This monastery was established in the 11th century and became a famous centre of learning of the Zhalu tradition instituted by Buton Rinchen Drub. It is also believed that this institution housed many Sanskrit texts.
19. Zhva lu. See: Zhva lu se khang, above.
20. Yer pa. A place of retreat on the top of Yerpa Lha Ri to the north-east of Lhasa. It is believed that this retreat place was founded by Mongsa Tsi Cham, one of the queens of King Songtsen Gampo.
21. gSang phu sne thong. The Sangphu monastery of Central Tibet built by Ngog Legpe Sherab, a disciple of Atisha, in the year 1073, and later renovated by Atisha's disciple Loden Sherab.
22. Fourteen transgressions. The 14 root downfalls or transgressions of the tantric vows are as follows: 1. Belittling the Vajra master; 2. Despising the precepts of the Buddha; 3. Speaking badly of Vajra brothers and sisters; 4. Abandoning love for sentient beings; 5. Abandoning the wishing and committed mind of enlightenment; 6. Despising the sutra and tantra teachings; 7. Exposing the secret of tantra to those who are not initiated; 8. Mistreating one's body; 9. Abandoning emptiness or being sceptical about it; 10. Associating with bad friends; 11. Not reflecting on emptiness; 12. Disturbing others' faith in the Dharma; 13. Not observing the pledges and commitments; and 14. Despising women.
23. Four kinds of enlightened activities. The peaceful, extensive, powerful and wrathful activities of an enlightened being, manifested to tame beings according to their mental disposition.